Praying the Passion
Living the Gospel

Scriptural Reflections for Adult Believers

Malcolm Cornwell, C.P.

Foreword by Donald Senior, C.P.

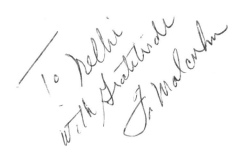

A Liturgical Press Book

THE LITURGICAL PRESS
Collegeville, Minnesota

Dedication

"Remember," Norman, my father, . . . "In baptism he died with Christ: may he also share his resurrection."

Eucharistic Prayer II

Cover design by Fred Petters

The Scripture quotations contained herein are from the New Revised Standard Version of the Bible, copyrighted, 1989 by the Division of Christian Education of the National Council of the Churches of Christ in the United States of America, and are used by permission. All rights reserved.

2   3   4   5   6   7   8   9

Library of Congress Cataloging-in-Publication Data

Cornwell, Malcolm, 1940–
    Praying the passion : living the Gospel—scriptural reflections for adult believers / Malcolm Cornwell.
        p.   cm.
    Includes bibliographical references.
    ISBN 0-8146-2220-8
    1. Jesus Christ—Passion—Meditations.   2. Lent—Prayer-books and devotions—English.   3. Church year meditations.   I. Title.
BT431.C67   1993
242'.34—dc20   92-40656
                                                                        CIP

Contents

Acknowledgements

Each work is much more than the thoughts of its author in print. It is a sign of the encouragement and assistance of many people. This book is no exception. I am grateful to the administration, faculty, and staff of the Catholic Theological Union in Chicago, as well as my own Passionist Community there for providing such a fine atmosphere for a sabbatical experience. I am especially indebted to Carroll Stuhlmueller, C.P., Joann Gehling, F.S.P.A., and Eloise Rosenblatt, R.S.M., for their input and assistance in the lands of the Bible. Thanks also to Dr. Wayne Rollins of Assumption College, Worcester, Massachusetts, who guided additional study for this book. To Dan Lewis who prepared the manuscript and to Bede Cameron, C.P., who proofread the text, I am most grateful. Finally, I must express gratitude to Dan Senger, O.F.M., and David Monaco, C.P., two friends who have each deepened my appreciation for the prayer traditions of our Franciscan/Passionist heritage.

Foreword

The Bible ignites when it is brought into contact with the living faith of the Church. While the tools of scholarship help unlock the meaning of the biblical text, the full force of the Bible is unleashed only when it touches human life as it struggles with the reality of God.

This book knows that well. Ultimately it is not a book about the Bible but a guide for those who wish to draw on the well of Scripture to give their prayer new meaning and force. The author taps powerful currents to achieve his goal. The biblical texts he concentrates on are some of the most dramatic and powerful segments of the New Testament, the Passion stories. He also draws on the liturgical year's most gripping moment: Holy Week and the Church's celebration of the death and resurrection of Jesus. Here as nowhere else in the Church's life, Scripture, liturgy, and personal prayer fuse.

While the passion stories are the terrain through which the reader is led, Malcolm Cornwell draws on a lifetime of pastoral experience as a preacher, retreat master, and spiritual guide to present each gospel account in an artful and reflective way. The respective accounts of Mark, Matthew, Luke, and John become enticing gateways into both the familiar sequence of the passion story and the perhaps less known but extraordinarily beautiful world of each evangelist's portrayal of Jesus. Thus with Mark's Gospel we sit at the Last Supper with Jesus and his disciples but also learn of Jesus' great ministry of healing and reconciliation, a ministry signified in Mark's Gospel in the breaking of the one bread. With Matthew we enter Gethsemane to witness Jesus' wrenching prayer and to brace for the arrest, and through Matthew's entire Gospel we learn the meaning of Jesus' prayerful bond of faith and love with God. We take the journey to Calvary with Luke's Gospel and learn how this enticing motif of the journey throughout the Gospel characterizes Luke's understanding of discipleship. And, finally, with John we stand by the cross as the Lamb of God triumphantly meets death and gives us life, fulfilling the destiny of the Word made flesh proclaimed on every page of John's Gospel.

The reader should be aware that I bring a prejudice to my appraisal of this work. Malcolm Cornwell, C.P, is a brother Passionist and I had the privilege of having him take a course on the passion narratives with me at Catholic Theological Union some years ago. But friendship aside, I am convinced the reader will find here a wonderful exploration of the world of prayer and the world of Scripture. True to its author's vocation as a preacher and spiritual guide, this is a book that does not forget and always respects its reader. It is clear, artful, and practical.

A book like this reminds me of the extraordinary treasures of our tradition: access to the profound beauty and power of the Scriptures; sustenance through a liturgical life drenched in symbol and transcendent beauty; a heritage of mystics and ordinary great saints who remind us that prayer is the lifebreath of our faith; and a gospel that dares to find

God's presence even in the midst of the cross death. Malcolm Cornwell embraces all of these powerful streams in this book and in so doing offers his readers something truly worthwhile.

Donald Senior, C.P.
Catholic Theological Union
Chicago, Illinois

Preface

Each year on Palm Sunday Christians throughout the world begin to observe what has come to be known as Holy Week. The week is holy because Jesus of Nazareth went up to Jerusalem, was crucified, and on the third day rose from the dead. Because of this, "God has made him both Lord and Messiah" (Acts 2:36). This is our faith and because it is our faith we make this annual spiritual pilgrimage in memory of these events in the life of Jesus.

Ever since the first Holy Week, pilgrims in the Christian journey have a distinct advantage over the first disciples of Jesus. We know and have experienced the results of the gospel story. Jesus is risen and his passion and death is a victory. Now we are able to remember and to celebrate these events with new eyes and new ears, for in our Holy Week celebrations we see and hear what Jesus' first disciples were not yet able to understand. John tells us, "His disciples did not understand these things at first; but when Jesus was glorified, then they remembered that these things had been written of him . . . " (John 12:16).

A Liturgical Pilgrim

From the very beginning of Christian times, pilgrims have gone in faith to the "holy places" connected with the passion, death, and resurrection of Jesus. We know this because shrines have marked the places connected with these events from the earliest times. During a recent sabbatical experience in Israel and other Bible lands I had the opportunity to experience in a deeper way the significance of these places and events. With the help of a book entitled "Diary of a Pilgrimage" and the four Gospels, I experienced the places and events of Christ's paschal mystery in a new and more prayerful way. The diary was written by a religious woman from Spain named Egeria. Sometime near the end of the fourth century she made a pilgrimage to the Holy Land and Jerusalem. Through her eyes we are invited to see the ceremonies that made up the Holy Week observance at that time. Through her ears we are encouraged to hear some of the scriptural readings and prayers that were part of the devotional and liturgical life of the Church at Jerusalem.

At the beginning of her description of Holy Week in Jerusalem, Egeria recalls that the people gathered in Bethany on the Saturday before Palm Sunday. This day was called the "Lazarus Saturday," and people went to Bethany in pilgrimage to remember the raising of this man to new life by Jesus. They also came to prepare for the rites and ceremonies of the "great" and "holy" week ahead. What is most interesting in this practice is the reading of John 12:1-11, a text that tells us that the events which follow, namely the anointing of Jesus by Mary and the procession of people who carried palms to greet Jesus on the following day, recorded in John 12:12-16, all took place "six days before the Passover" (John 12:1). It was through the proclamation of this text that the Jerusalem community and visiting pilgrims like Egeria were encouraged to prepare, not only to remember the events of Jesus' last week before his death and resurrection, but also to celebrate the effects of these "saving mysteries" in their lives once again.

Praying the Passion

Some form of meditation on the passion of Jesus has always been part of our Christian tradition and devotion. From the time of Apostle Paul, who reflectively wrote, "The life I now live in the flesh I live by faith in the Son of God who loved me and gave himself for me" (Gal 2:20), until the present day, followers of Christ have found strength and inspiration in the gospel story of Jesus' passion, death, and resurrection. Today with the revival of a biblical and liturgical spirituality there is still a need and desire to continue the practice of a prayerful devotion to the passion of Christ. This devotion, however, needs to be in harmony with the spirit of the liturgy and the insights of contemporary biblical scholarship.

Personal meditation and reflection on the passion of Jesus is suitable at any time but it is especially so during the season of Lent. This season is a call to the entire faith community of Christian believers to renewal of life through personal conversion aided by prayer and fasting, penance and good works and meditation on the passion of the Lord. Each year I am struck that this rhythm is reflected at the very outset of our Lenten observance. On Ash Wednesday, the Church invites us to "Turn away from sin and be faithful to the gospel" with the prayer for the imposition of ashes on our foreheads. The next day the Church invites us to begin reflection on the passion of Jesus and our call to follow him in faithful discipleship through the reading of one of the predictions of his passion (Roman Lectionary no. 221, Luke 9:22-25). Gospel living and prayerful reflection on the paschal mystery reflect the plan of the liturgy for our growth in Christ during Lent or any season of life.

Living the Gospel

The gospel story looks back at Jesus in the light of his rising from the dead. The Gospels help us to understand that as the early Christians reflected on Jesus they came to "see" and "hear" him in a new way. That new "seeing" and "hearing" is the experience we now call faith. This faith is not merely a set of learned truths; it is a life of commitment and celebration. Through prayerful reflection on the passion of Jesus and the liturgy of Holy Week we are called once again to "see" and "hear" Jesus in a new way as we celebrate our faith commitment to him. We do this in a way and at a depth that his first disciples never fully understood or experienced until he was raised from the dead.

Today our renewed liturgy combines with a time-honored tradition to give special significance to prayer and reflection on the passion, death, and resurrection of Jesus during Holy Week. The central focus for the liturgy of Passion Sunday is the solemn proclamation of the passion of our Lord Jesus Christ. The narrative selected is one of the Synoptic Gospels as designated by the three-year cycle of the Lectionary. Later in the week, Good Friday gives primacy of place to the passion narrative from the Gospel of John. Thus both Lent and Holy Week, as well as a time-honored tradition of Christian devotion, encourage us to prayerfully reflect on the meaning of the gospel message in the light of Christ's paschal mystery.

In an earlier volume, *Arise and Renew,* I concentrated on the gospel narratives of the resurrection and the Lectionary selections from the Gospel of John for the Easter season. Encouraged by readers and friends, I have now turned to the narratives of Christ's passion for insights into the message of each of the Gospels. Inspired by the recent studies of several scholars and my own sabbatical experience in Israel, I have tried to reflect contemporary scholarship as well as traditional and liturgical spirituality in these gospel reflections. I am especially indebted to my confrere and mentor,

Donald Senior, for both his professional insights and personal encouragement. In some small way, I hope I have brought the heights of his scriptural expertise into the depths of spiritual experience through these scriptural reflections and prayer exercises.

A Guide for Prayer

This book has one purpose in mind: to aid adult believers in praying the gospel message with special emphasis on the narratives of Christ's passion. To assist us in this prayerful reflection the Church invites us to use the season of Lent as a time of meditative preparation for the events of Holy Week. Also, throughout the history of spirituality, people like the Apostle Paul, Francis of Assisi, Catherine of Siena, and Paul of the Cross have urged Christian believers to ponder the love of God revealed in the passion of Jesus. It is my own hope that the reflections that follow will open many hearts to the depths contained in the narratives that gave rise to the entire gospel message.

With these thoughts in mind I offer the following reflections on gospel life based on significant scenes from the passion narratives. At the end of each reflection I will provide some practical guidance for a variety of personal prayer experiences. I will also recommend further reading for continued reflection and prayer. I do this with the hope of fostering not only a deeper love for the passion narratives themselves, but more especially a passion for prayer and a deeper desire for gospel living.

Malcolm Cornwell, C.P.
Feast of St. Paul of the Cross

Chapter 1

"Hosanna!"
An Initial Reflection

At the beginning of the Palm Sunday celebration we recall Christ's entry into Jerusalem amid shouts of "Hosanna." This event is found in all the Gospels. The Gospel of John reflects on it in the passage John 12:12-16. I recommend reading it.

Seeing and Hearing the Lord
As we recall this event through the text of John, we see Jesus' entrance into Jerusalem amid a mood of contrast and conflict. We hear the crowd shout praise to Jesus, but we also know that the chief priests have plotted to kill him because many people began to turn to him in faith after he raised Lazarus from the dead (John 12:10-11). For the moment, the cheers of the crowd seem to drown out the conflict surrounding Jesus. We hear only shouts of praise. Hosanna! John paints such a vivid picture.

The crowds have come out to Bethany and the Mount of Olives to greet Jesus as the "King of Israel" (John 12:13). The people wave palm and olive branches in Jesus' honor as he passes. Jesus seems to accept this praise as the crowds continue to acclaim their king, a title he has tried to avoid up to this point in John's Gospel. For John, Jesus is indeed a king, but not a conquering hero-king; instead, he is a servant-leader who enters Jerusalem not on a mighty stallion, but on a lowly donkey. What we see contrasts with what we hear, and this adds to the mounting sense of conflict.

As we recall the event of Jesus' entry into Jerusalem, we hear the crowd give voice to Israel's praise of a conquering hero-king. "Bind the festal procession with branches . . . ," for "Blessed is the one who comes in the name of the Lord" (Ps 118:27, 26). To this ancient song of praise, John adds the accolade, "the King of Israel" (John 12:13). But the Jesus we see is far from the image of a conquering king: we see the Jesus who "found a young donkey and sat upon it" as it is written, "Look, your king is coming sitting on a donkey's colt" (John 12:14-15). While Jesus accepts the acclaim of the crowd, he does it in the image of the bearer of peace foretold by the prophet Zechariah, "Rejoice . . . your king comes to you, triumphant and victorious is he, humble and riding on a donkey" (Zech 9:9).

Jesus and Lazarus

Once before in the story of John's Gospel the crowds were ready to acclaim Jesus as their king. It was after the event of the feeding of the multitudes, another sign Jesus performed for the crowds to see and hear. But then, Jesus was not ready to be hailed as their king (John 6:15). Now, Jesus seems willing to accept the crowd's acclaim since he is ready to become their king, but on a level and in a way they will only understand after he is risen from the dead. Jesus' reign as king will not renew national domination for

Israel; rather, it will usher in an era of peace for all the nations. For John, Jesus is the kingly-servant of Zechariah's prophecy who "shall command peace to the nations" (Zech 9:10). Through this image of Jesus as a humble bearer of peace to the nations, John wants us to see and hear Jesus as the "King of Israel" (John 12:13).

There is joy and excitement in the crowd not only because of Jesus, but also because of Lazarus "whom he had raised from the dead" (John 12:1, 9). The sign of the risen Lazarus alive and with them was something the crowds could see and hear. Lazarus was once dead; they had seen him in the tomb. Now he was alive, they had heard Jesus call him to new life. This sign was the final reason for the crowd to acclaim Jesus as king.

For those who have eyes to see and ears to hear, John's linkage of Jesus' entry into Jerusalem with his visit to Bethany to be with the risen Lazarus whom the crowds came out to see (John 12:9), is John's great prologue to the "Book of Glory" and the story of Jesus' passion. There John will proclaim that Jesus is indeed a king. As believing Christians beginning to pray the message of the gospel in the light of Christ's passion, we too come out "to see Lazarus" and in him we find the meaning of the kingdom Jesus has come to proclaim. In Lazarus our brother, we find the gifts Jesus bestows on all who believe in him; in Lazarus we find light and life (John 12:9, 17-18).

A Day in Bethany

The diary of Egeria tells us that people went out to Bethany on the Saturday before Holy Week to commemorate the raising of Lazarus and to recall Jesus' visit to Lazarus and his sisters. At present in our Lectionary readings we recall these events on the Monday of Holy Week with the text of John 12:1-11, but the continual reflection on these events either before or after Palm Sunday shows us that the person of the risen Lazarus and his sisters Martha and Mary are key figures in the memory and celebration of these days and events. In John 12:1-11 Lazarus is twice mentioned as the one Jesus had raised from the dead (John 12:1, 9). In the actual story of Lazarus' being raised from the dead to new life, both Martha and Mary play an important part. Though filled with grief they both believe that Jesus' presence would have made a difference. If Jesus had been there, Lazarus would not have died (John 11:21, 32). Mary knelt at his feet and Martha even said she believed Jesus was the "Messiah, the Son of God" (John 11:27, 32). In the other Gospels, this is the faith of the Church pronounced by Peter (Mark 8:29; Matt 16:16; Luke 9:20).

In the scene of John 12:1-11, "six days before the Passover," Martha and Mary and Lazarus and a growing crowd of believers gather around Jesus at a meal in the home of Lazarus. This is a sign of their growing loyalty to him. In stark contrast and as a sign of the mounting conflict, the Sanhedrin also gathers, but this meeting is to plot the death of Jesus (John 12:9-11). In the midst of this scene of contrast and conflict, Mary, the sister of the risen Lazarus, approaches Jesus to kneel at his feet once again. At first she knelt before him to proclaim her faith. Now that faith prompts her to an act of loving service. "Mary took a pound of costly perfume made of pure nard, anointed Jesus' feet, and wiped them with her hair. The house was filled with the fragrance of the perfume" (John 12:3).

This dramatic gesture is filled with deep meaning. Anointing of feet is an act of humble adoration, yet Mary's perfumed oil is fit for a king and its odor penetrates the entire room. No wonder that when Judas protested such waste no one paid attention to his words. Instead it is the word of Jesus that gives meaning to this extravagant gesture. He said the anointing was "for the day of my burial" (John 12:7). This comment declared Mary's gesture to be a prophetic action. The anointing prefigured his kingly burial in death, just as the procession with palms and praise looked ahead to his final enthronement on the cross. John will reveal this later in his dramatic account of Christ's passion of Good Friday; for now he simply reminds us that it is through death and resurrection that Jesus will become King and Lord of Life for all who believe in him.

Prayer and Pilgrimage

Mary, Martha, and Lazarus are signs to us of true loyalty and faith in Christian discipleship as once again we join the multitudes of pilgrims and believers who have gone before us to recall in faith what Jesus said and did at Bethany, Jerusalem, and Calvary. Like Mary, we have heard the voice of Jesus call her brother to new life. In the words "Lazarus, come out" (John 11:43) we have all heard our common call to newness of life in Christ. And like Mary, this new life prompts us to acts of faith and gestures of loving service in the name of Jesus, the risen Lord.

In the Gospel of John, the story of the anointing of Jesus by Mary in the presence of Martha and her resurrected brother Lazarus precedes the solemn entry of Jesus into Jerusalem. These events, "six days before the passover" (John 12:1), are a turning point in the Gospel of John and a fitting point to begin our prayerful reflections on the message of the Gospels and Christ's passion. Like loyal disciples of every age, we gather in faith to remember and to celebrate these events as we prepare to "see" and "hear" once again what Jesus' first disciples came to understand only after he had been raised from the dead (John 12:16).

Prayer Exercises

The Raising of Lazarus and the Plot to Kill Jesus (John 11:17-53)

"It is better for you to have one man die for the people than to have the whole nation destroyed" (John 11:50). The one who will die is Jesus, who declared, "I am the Resurrection and the Life" (John 11:25). Talk with Jesus about how he has been resurrection and life for you, perhaps even in the face of death. Like Martha, make your own act of faith in the Lord.

The Meal at Bethany (John 12:1-11)

Mary, Martha, Lazarus, and Jesus are at table together. Choose one of these people and dialogue with them about the events that will soon unfold. Ask the person you select to journey with you as you begin your prayer experience with the passion of Christ. What advice or encouragement does the person offer as you begin your prayer journey with Christ to Calvary? Pray about what they say.

Jesus' Entry into Jerusalem (John 12:12-19)

Jesus comes humbly on a donkey, yet the crowds recognize his power to raise people to new life. Pray to recognize that power in your own life. As you pray, remember the words of Jesus, "For this reason the Father loves me, because I lay down my life, in order to take it up again" (John 10:17). How does the pattern of Jesus' dying and rising manifest itself in your life? As you experience this mystery are you able to pray, "Blessed is the one who comes in the name of the Lord" (Ps 118:26)?

Recommended Reading

Flanagan, Neal M., O.F.M. *The Gospel According to John and the Johannine Epistles.* Collegeville Bible Commentary. Collegeville, Minn.: The Liturgical Press, 1982.

Gingras, George E., ed. *Egeria. Diary of a Pilgrimage.* Ancient Christian Writers 38. New York: Newman Press, 1970.

Haenchen, Ernst. *A Commentary of the Gospel of John.* Philadelphia, Pa.: Fortress Press, 1984.

McPolin, James, S.J. *John.* New Testament Message. Wilmington, Del.: Michael Glazier, Inc., 1982.

Senior, Donald, C.P. *The Passion of Jesus in the Gospel of John.* Collegeville, Minn.: The Liturgical Press, A Michael Glazier Book, 1991.

Taylor, Michael J., S.J. *John, The Different Gospel.* New York: Alba House, 1983.

Chapter 2

"At the Table"
Mark's Challenge to Servant Discipleship

Dining with friends is a sign of kinship. In the Gospel of Mark, Jesus' dining with outcasts and sinners is a sign of God's in-breaking kingdom. Throughout the Gospel of Mark there are scenes in which Jesus eats with or provides food for various groups of people (see Mark 2:15-17; 6:34-44; 8:1-10; 14:3-9; 14:12-25).

The story sequence of Mark's Gospel is punctuated by several structural markings or inclusions; namely, events or stories or descriptions of similar motifs that surround an inner core of narrative material. These inclusions highlight and give deeper meaning to the inner section of the narrative. This is evident in the section between the two healings of blind men (8:22-26 and 10:46-52) where the inner section of narrative (8:27–10:45) describes the increasing blindness of the disciples to the challenge of Jesus' impending suffering and death. This same type of inclusion motif is found in the Gospel's structure regarding the stories of Jesus' meals with sinners and outcasts, the feeding of vast multitudes, even the final meal in the intimate circle of his disciples. In the meal and feeding scenes of Mark's Gospel Jesus manifests both kinship and kingdom in the inclusive motif of table fellowship.

Table Fellowship: An Inclusive Motif

A MEAL WITH LEVI, THE TAX COLLECTOR (2:13-17)

Early in Mark's Gospel Jesus calls Levi, a tax collector, to follow him (2:14). Immediately after this invitation to discipleship, Mark tells us that Jesus "sat at dinner in Levi's house" where "many tax collectors and sinners were also sitting with Jesus and his disciples—for there were many who followed him" (2:15). This and similar scenes of table fellowship are expressive of the inner core of the gospel message. Jesus' bold gesture of welcoming or accepting invitations to table fellowship with outcasts and sinners was a shocking yet compelling expression of God's inclusion of those outside the Jewish community into the saving experience of the kingdom of God.

A MEAL WITH SIMON THE LEPER (14:3-9)

Immediately before the scene of the final meal with his disciples in Mark's Gospel, Jesus accepts an invitation to dine in the home of a man referred to as Simon the leper. Nothing is known of this Simon, whether he was cured earlier by Jesus or was still afflicted. The fact that Jesus associated with him and "sat at the table" with him is another sign of Jesus' inclusion of outcasts into his ministry of table fellowship.

Another person is mentioned as being with Jesus in this table scene. "A woman came with an alabaster jar of very costly ointment of nard, and she broke open the jar and poured the ointment on his head" (14:3b). No word is given regarding her background or identity, but question is made about her extravagance. "Why was the ointment wasted in this way?" (14:4). Jesus comes to her defense. "Let her alone," he says, "Why do you trouble her?" "She has done what she could, she has anointed my body beforehand for its burial" (14:6, 8).

Earlier at the meal in the home of Levi and his fellow tax collectors, question was also made about Jesus ' behavior at table. "Why does he eat with tax collectors and sinners?" (2:16). There Jesus had replied, "Those who are well have no need of a physician, but those who are sick; I have come to call not the righteous but sinners" (2:17).

In both meal scenes Mark portrays Jesus as exercising a ministry towards outcasts and sinners. These scenes, placed at the outset and near the conclusion of the Gospel, serve to highlight the inner core of Mark's message. Between Jesus' assertion of the meaning of his mission as a call to sinners, and the fact of his impending death anticipated by his anointing as an invitation to share in his passion, Mark unfolds the drama of his gospel message. The inclusion of this message between scenes of table fellowship alert a reflective reader to levels of deeper meaning in the scenes depicting Jesus eating with or feeding others.

A FINAL MEAL WITH THE DISCIPLES (14:22-31)

In the ancient Near East the intimacy of table fellowship was and is a manifest sign of hospitality, trust, even reconciliation. Several examples occur in the Hebrew Scriptures (see Gen 18:1-8; 26:30; 2 Kgs 25:27-29). Later in Wisdom and Prophetic literature the meal took on the added notes of a sign of final bonding in wisdom with God (see Prov 9:1-6; Isa 55:1-3). To be disloyal or to take advantage of someone's hospitality to betray them was considered the most despicable of sins (see 2 Sam 13:23-29; 1 Macc 16: 15-19). The psalmist bemoans the very thought of betrayal from a trusted companion with the verse, "Even my bosom friend in whom I trusted, who ate of my bread, has lifted the heel against me" (Ps 41:9).

Mark includes the motif of betrayal in the scene of the final meal Jesus celebrated with his disciples. The very table at which Jesus bonds with his disciples for a last fellowship meal (14:22-25) is surrounded not only with his closest companions (14:17, 20), but with thoughts of betrayal (14:17-21) and denial (14:26-31).

Through a series of structural inclusions, Mark draws our attention to the central message of his gospel narrative. Jesus' mission is a call to sinners and outcasts. His passion and death are not only a personal destiny, but an invitation to his disciples to a deeper commitment to service in union with him. This mission and this destiny are portrayed and explained through Jesus' word and deed during the various meal or feeding episodes recorded in Mark's Gospel. Though important, the "Last Supper" is one meal in a series of meals or feeding events in which Mark reflects on the challenge of Jesus' ministry of table fellowship and the call to follow him in loyal servant discipleship.

Feeding the Multitudes: An Inclusive Ministry

All four of the evangelists recall the story of the feeding of the multitudes, an event which obviously left a lasting impression on the early Christian communities. Mark has two accounts of the event and structures them to develop a theme of inclusive ministry to both Jew and Gentile. This becomes obvious to an alert reader, but the disciples appear blind to this development as the gospel story progresses. A reflection on this section of Mark's Gospel will help to see this development and to hear its message.

BREAD AND BLINDNESS (6:31–8:26)

This section of the central portion of Mark's Gospel begins with an invitation of Jesus for the disciples to "come away to a deserted place" to "rest" and "eat" (6:31), and ends with Jesus laying his hands upon a blind man for a healing. At Jesus' repeated touch of the man, "his sight was restored, and he saw everything clearly" (8:25). Throughout this section the reader is invited to see the meaning of Jesus' mission as an expression of his inclusive ministry to both Jew and Gentile.

Taken as a unit, this section of Mark's Gospel is a challenge to the reader to see and hear the meaning and message of the feeding ministry of Jesus. It is another expression of Jesus' invitation to participate in the ministry of table fellowship. The challenge to see and hear its meaning is summed up in Jesus' dramatic questions: "How many baskets full of broken pieces did you collect? . . . Do you not yet understand?" (8:19, 20, 21). Before we attempt to wrestle with the answers to these questions about the meaning of the bread, it will be helpful to reflect on some of the events contained in this section, and the feeding stories in particular.

THE FIRST FEEDING STORY (6:30-44)

Jesus invites his disciples to a desert place to rest and eat. A crowd follows them and the scene is set for a teaching in word and deed. The desert was a place of testing, yet strangely a place of feeding (Exod 16:32). Jesus the caring shepherd has compassion on the crowd, yet challenges his disciples to provide for their hunger when they suggest he send the multitudes away to buy food. Jesus responds, "You give them something to eat" (6:37). They provide him with a meager five loaves and two fish. Like the gracious shepherd of Israel, Jesus does not desire his followers to "want" for nourishment, so he instructs them to "lie down in green pastures" where he "prepares a table" before them (see Ps 23:1, 2, 5).

The people gather in groups of hundreds and fifties. Despite the deserted atmosphere and the allusions to the struggles during the Exodus, the crowd gathers like Israel of old in community groupings to recline for a meal in a place of fertile refreshment. The image is of a renewed Israel cared for and fed by Jesus their new shepherd. This allusion to Israel is strengthened by the gathering of the twelve baskets of fragments after the crowd is fed.

While it looks back to Israel and its life in the desert, this scene may also look forward to the Church and its life in community, especially in its gathering for Eucharistic table fellowship. There are many allusions to our gatherings for the Eucharist in this feeding account. Jesus "takes, blesses, breaks and gives" the bread to his disciples (see 6:41). He also does this at the final meal before his passion (see Mark 14:22). The small numbers in the groupings of hundreds and fifties seem to reflect the first modest gatherings of Christians for Eucharist in the early days of the Church. Even the fragments gathered in a "Jewish style" basket after the feeding are described by a word used to designate the Eucharist in later liturgical usage.

THE CROSSING OF THE LAKE (6:45-52)

Between the two feeding scenes, 6:34-44 and 8:1-10, there is the story of the difficult crossing of the storm-tossed Lake of Galilee. Mark's account of this incident is filled with allusions to the Exodus event. Jesus comes to the distressed disciples walking on and calming the water. He appears as if "he intended to pass them by," but when he speaks he declares "It is I." When Jesus climbs into the boat with the disciples "they were utterly astounded, for they did not understand about the loaves" (see 6:48, 49, 50, 52). Only God has such mastery over the waters (Gen 1:1-10). Only the "I Am" of Israel has the power to make the seas passable and calm (Exod 3:14; 14:21). Only the Lord of Israel sheltered Moses in the hollow of the rock until he passed by (Exod 32:22). Now Jesus is protecting his own new Israel with his presence. Wind, water, and wayfaring hearts all become calm in the presence of the one who says, "It is I; do not be afraid" (6:50).

THE SECOND FEEDING STORY (8:1-10)

The second feeding episode takes place after the difficult crossing of the stormy Lake of Galilee. According to Mark we are now in Gentile territory. The tone and the style of this story have their own flavor. Actually, the feeding event may have occurred only once, but in Mark's narrative the two stories express different messages about the meaning of the mission of Jesus.

In this story, Jesus takes the initiative to feed the crowd who has been with him now for three days. The disciples still do not seem to understand and so they protest, "How can one feed these people with bread here in the desert?" (8:4) While the first feeding story was more pastoral in tone with meditative allusions to Psalm 23, this second episode seems more missionary in tone with reference to people who "have come from a great distance." They must be fed before their return home, otherwise "they will faint on the way" (8:3).

Again, overtones of the Eucharist are present. Jesus performs the consistent ritual gestures for the blessing and breaking of the bread (see 8:6). Here, however, the number of the loaves and baskets has changed. The number seven for the "Gentile style" containers of the gathered fragments may well indicate a universal dimension to the mission of Jesus.

Mark draws attention to these differences in the feeding stories so the reader-disciple can begin to see what the first disciples failed to understand. Jesus' mission is universal. He embraces both Jew and Gentile. Indeed, all are called to find nourishment in him, even at the meal of Eucharistic table fellowship. For Mark, Jesus is meant to be "one loaf" for all.

ONE LOAF—ONE MISSION—ONE VISION (8:13-21)

As the disciples cross the lake once again to return home they have only "one loaf" in the boat (8:14). Jesus now puts the disciples through an intense interrogation. In a series of hammering questions, he asks them about the meaning of the loaves, chiding them as he does so: "Are your hearts hardened?" "Do you have eyes and fail to see?" "Do you have ears and fail to hear?" (8:17b, 18). The conclusions to these inquiries become clearer to the reader-disciple despite the deafness and blindness of the first disciples to Jesus' message.

The most difficult crossing is not that of a storm-tossed lake; the most difficult of crossings is to a change of outlook, to a new understanding of Jesus' mission and a new vision of his ministry. To follow Jesus is to see his mission and to hear his message in a new way. It is a universal call to Jew and Gentile alike, a call to life in God through Jesus' inclusive invitation to Eucharistic table fellowship.

At the end of the section beginning with the first feeding, Jesus healed a deaf man (7:31-37). Now, as this section of Mark's Gospel concludes, Jesus heals a blind man (8:22-26). Though the reader sees and hears Jesus more clearly, the disciples are still in darkness and incomprehension, left to ponder Jesus' haunting questions:

> "Do you not remember? . . . "
> "When I broke the five loaves for the five thousand, how many baskets full of broken pieces did you collect?"
> "And the seven for the four thousand, how many baskets full . . . did you collect?"
> "Do you not yet understand?" (8:18, 19, 20, 21)

The memory of the disciples seems dull and their understanding incomplete.

THE CUP AND PASSIONATE VISION (8:22–10:52)

This part of the central portion of Mark's Gospel begins and ends with the healing of a person who is blind. Immediately following the first healing (8:22-26) we encounter a series of episodes that move the reader closer to Jerusalem. During this journey Jesus will allude to his sufferings several times and pose a challenge to his disciples regarding his passion. He invites them not only to see the challenge of the passion, but to share in his commitment to it. By the themes of bread and blindness Mark has led his reader to the midpoint of his story and the climactic confession of Peter that Jesus is the Messiah (8:29). Now, as the story continues, Jesus will lead his followers to the painful conclusion that his final glory is by way of total service, much suffering, and finally death.

Three Predictions of the Passion

The first prediction of the passion (8:31) is immediately followed by a challenge to the disciples to "deny themselves and take up their cross and follow me" (8:34). In each of the subsequent predictions of his passion we discover the same links with faithful discipleship. To follow Jesus is to walk the way of self-sacrifice and service to others. The second passion prediction (9:30-31) is quickly linked with further challenges to fidelity and dedication: "Whoever wants to be first must be last of all and servant of all" (9:35). The third prediction of the passion (10:32-34) is immediately followed by the request of James and John for primacy of place in Jesus' kingdom. Accenting their misunderstanding of his call to service Jesus quickly challenges their desires with the haunting question, "Are you able to drink the cup that I drink?" (10:38), and concludes with the climactic reason for his mission and ministry: "The Son of Man came not to be served, but to serve, and to give his life as a ransom for many" (10:45). Jesus is truly the servant Messiah.

For Mark, Jesus' true identity is expressed in his life-giving death. To recognize Jesus as the suffering servant who gives his life for the many is the key to clear vision and new life. This is the message of Mark's journey narrative and his teaching on discipleship and the passion of Jesus. Mark surrounds this entire section with the healing of blindness in the hope that, like Bartimaeus, the reader-disciple will follow Jesus both in faith and commitment to his destiny in Jerusalem. There Jesus and his disciples will eat the Passover (14:12) and Jesus will drink the cup that is prepared for him (14:36).

Eucharistic Fellowship: An Inclusive Challenge

The motif of inclusion reaches a climatic impact in Mark's account of the Passover. Chapter 14 of Mark's Gospel begins, "It was two days before the Passover . . ." (14:1). The scene of the supper concludes with Jesus' words of interpretation of the bread and cup: "Take; this is my body. . . . This is my blood of the Covenant, which is poured out for many" (14:22, 24). Once again, story and structure come together to convey Mark's message.

Throughout Mark's Gospel, outcasts and sinners, multitudes both Jewish and Gentile have enjoyed table fellowship with Jesus. In all of these episodes both reader and disciples were invited to see and hear the meaning of Jesus' mission. Now on the eve of his passion both reader and disciples are re-invited to sit with him at table in the intimate setting of his final Passover in Eucharistic table fellowship.

JESUS' FINAL MEAL (14:12-31)

Eucharist is not only bread, blessed and broken; Eucharist is also cup poured out and shared. Together they are a symbol of Christ's passion and a sign of the bond he has established with his disciples. With these thoughts in mind we begin the celebration of Jesus' last meal. "When it was evening, he came with the twelve . . . they had taken their places and were eating" (14:17, 18).

In the midst of the familial setting of Jesus eating with his friends, not outcasts, not sinners, not Gentile or Jewish crowds, but friends and intimate companions, Jesus injects a stabbing note of tragic sorrow:

> "I tell you, *one of you* will betray me, one who is eating with me" (14:18).

> "It is *one of the twelve,* one who is dipping bread into the bowl with me" (14:20).

The plotting of betrayal in the course of a fellowship meal is the deepest breach of table fellowship. It is the dreaded image of the psalmist, "Even my bosom friend who ate my bread has lifted the heel against me" (Ps 41:9).

Jesus the Son of Man is about to give his life as a ransom for many, as was written of him. Long ago Isaiah wrote of the Lord's servant who would make the people righteous and bear the sins of many (Isa 53:11, 12). Quietly, calmly, almost majestically, Jesus sits at table, takes the bread, and cup, says the blessings, breaks the bread and gives the cup to those at table with him. This fellowship is like no other known before, for the bread is now "my body"; the cup is now "my blood of the covenant" (14:22, 24).

The prayerful reader shares this invitation to fellowship with Jesus in discipleship, in mission, and in passionate commitment to others. We sit at table with Jesus seeing and hearing the word and deed of table fellowship, while growing in the dawning awareness that the bread and the cup are more than Eucharist. They are signs of our universal mission and our total service to the many for whom Jesus has given himself in life, in passion, and in death.

Reflection in Prayer

Unlike the conclusion to the previous feeding stories, Jesus now asks no questions. Here in the intimate setting of Eucharistic fellowship, Jesus asks no questions about understanding the meaning of the bread, no questions about remembering those he has fed, no questions about loyalty in discipleship or commitment in mission. Instead he simply speaks of bread and cup, their total identification with himself, his sacrifice, and his service, and the challenge they pose to loyal disciples. Here the challenge is not, can we eat the bread, can we drink the cup? The true challenge is that of faithfulness and loyalty and service to others. Through Mark's ultimate inclusion (14:18, 20), he indicates the possibility of betrayal even within the inner circle of Jesus' chosen disciples and intimate friends. Even at the table of Eucharistic fellowship we can not quiet the haunting and terrifying question as it pierces the night air and the inner silence of our hearts: "Surely, not I?" (14:19). Prayerfully, yet painfully, the question still remains.

Prayer Exercises

Prayer at Table

- The meal with Levi (2:13-17)
- The meal with Simon, the leper (14:3-9)
- The meal with the disciples (14:22-31)

Choose one of these table scenes for reflection. Enter into the mind of the group at table with Jesus. Who do you identify with in the story? Why? What do you say to Jesus about your life situation while sharing in table fellowship with him? What does he say to you? Reflect on this scene with this saying of Jesus in mind: "The time is fulfilled, and the kingdom of God has come near, repent and believe in the good news" (1:15).

THE FIRST FEEDING STORY (6:30-44)

Three elements in this story seem to set the mood—rest, refreshment, and a deserted place. Pray with Jesus about your attitudes concerning the need for rest, refreshment, and solitude in your life. As an active person how does the rhythm of the apostolic call described in the Gospel play itself out in your life? "He named apostles, to be with him, and to be sent out to proclaim the message" (3:14). Talk to Jesus about your experience of being with him.

Now pray Psalm 23, describing the ministry of the compassionate shepherd. Re-read the feeding story in Mark 6:30-44. What connections do you make between the ministry of the shepherd in the psalm and the activity of Jesus in the story? Discuss with Jesus your own sense of compassion toward those to whom you minister. Pray or write out your own psalm/prayer of compassion in ministry.

THE SECOND FEEDING STORY (8:1-10).

The mood of this story is different. People have come a great distance to be with Jesus and hear his words. Pray about Jesus' willingness to include strangers in his company. How do you welcome/respond to strangers? Ask Jesus to teach you about his desire for all to be fed and nourished in him. What attitudes need to change in you for you to be a more effective witness to Jesus' mission of universal salvation? How do Jesus' words about vision affect you? "Do you have eyes and fail to see?" (8:18).

Predictions of the Passion (8:34; 9:31; 10:32-34)

CALL TO SERVICE (10:35-45)

Jesus not only speaks of his passion, he invites others to share in it. "Are you able to drink the cup that I drink . . . ?" (10:38). That is Jesus' big question. How have you shared in the cup of Jesus' passion in your own life? In the lives of others? Talk with Jesus about these events. How have you grown in a spirit of servanthood through these moments of sharing in Jesus' passion?

THE FINAL MEAL (14:12-31)

The mood of this meal is one of intimate company with trusted friends. This makes Jesus' words, "One of you will betray me" all the more jarring (14:18). Jesus has shared table fellowship with outcasts and sinners, fed large numbers of Jews and Gentiles, and never spoken of betrayal. Yet in the company of intimate friends and companions he speaks of disloyalty and treachery. How does this make you feel? What personal betrayals do you need to talk to Jesus about? How do you respond as Jesus continues to offer you his bread with the words, "Take, this is my body" (14:22), and the cup with the words, "This is my blood of the covenant which is poured out for many" (14:24)?

Remember, these words are spoken by a Jesus who has told his most intimate companions, "The Son of Man came not to be served, but to serve . . . " (10:45). Pray with Jesus about your own call to servant discipleship.

Recommended Reading

Barta, K. *The Gospel of Mark*. Wilmington, Del.: Michael Glazier, 1988.

Harrington, Wilfrid, O.P. *Mark*. Wilmington, Del.: Michael Glazier, 1979.

LaVerdiere, Eugene, S.S.S. "In Hundreds and Fifties." *Emmanuel* October 1985.

_____. "The Evening of the Third Day." *Emmanuel* November 1985.

_____. "The Breaking of Bread." *Emmanuel* December 1989.

Mann, C.S. *Mark*. The Anchor Bible. Garden City, N.Y.: Doubleday and Co., 1986.

Schnackenburg, Rudolf. *The Gospel According to Mark*. 2 vols. New York: Crossroad, 1981.

Senior, Donald, C.P. *The Passion of Jesus in the Gospel of Mark*. Wilmington, Del.: Michael Glazier, 1982.

Stock, Augustine, O.S.B. *Call to Discipleship: A Literary Study of Mark's Gospel*. Wilmington, Del.: Michael Glazier, 1982.

Van Linden, Philip, C.M. *The Gospel According to Mark*. Collegeville, Minn.: The Liturgical Press, 1982.

Chapter 3

"In the Garden"
Matthew's Portrait of
Jesus' Gethsemane Lament

    Lament is a rich and time-honored form of prayer. It is found in many of the psalms, especially those that express the plight of the one praying. The intent of the prayer of lament is not so much to explain the contradiction, pain, or difficulty of the one praying, but rather simply to place the dilemma before God. Whether we are experiencing illness, the dread of impending death, personal betrayal, or misfortune of any kind, our lament is the honest placing of this dilemma before the Lord in prayer.

    Walter Brueggemann writes in *Praying the Psalms* that lament is "disorientation addressed to God," and that in the address something happens to modify the disorientation. The prayer of lament creates a bond of acknowledgment between the one praying and God. It is, according to Brueggemann, a type of "grief work," a kind of self-therapy that gives objectivity to the cause of the disorientation before God, thus making it possible to deal with it. Prayerful lament expresses our human pain, grief, and dismay, even our anger that life is not good, but it also "refuses to settle for things as they are."

Lament also asserts a notion of hope. This type of prayer, especially as it is found in the psalms of lament, helps us to see that our contact with God is not meant to be business as usual. By linking our experience of disorientation with a prayerful stance before God through the use of a psalm of lament, we will discover, according to Brueggemann, "that the psalm is affected by our experience, and even more surprising, we find that our experience has been dealt with by the psalm."

A Psalm of Lament

Psalm 42–43 is a psalm of lament; most likely it was the prayer of an individual forced to live away from Jerusalem. Perhaps it is a prayer from the time of the Exile or simply the expression of someone in anguish because of his or her longing for the sight of the Temple. The psalm is clearly divided into three parts.

PSALM 42:1-5

The first section describes the situation of an unspecified anxiety. The one at prayer feels deep anguish, stating, "my tears have been my food day and night." Taunters cry out, "Where is your God?" Yet by recalling the joys of the Temple festivals the one at prayer has a ray of light and hope in God.

PSALM 42:6-11

The second section simply re-emphasizes the plight of the one praying. Deep anguish overtakes the one at prayer. There is a feeling of agony, a near death anguish, and a sense of abandonment by God. "Deep calls to deep . . . all your waves and your billows have gone over me." "I say to God, my rock, 'Why have you forgotten me?'"

PSALM 43:1-5

In the third and final section of the psalm, the one praying makes an appeal to God, a plea for deliverance, "Vindicate me, O God," and then concludes with a note of hope—a certainty of praising God again.

Each of the three sections of the psalm end with a common refrain.

> "Why are you cast down, O my soul?
> Why are you disquieted within me?
> Hope in God. For I shall again praise him, my help and my God"
> (Ps 42:5, 11; 43:5).

This refrain seems to highlight each of the three sections, giving an emphasis to the tone of each part of the psalm. As you pray the psalm you may wish to concenteate on the first line of the refrain for the initial section of the psalm, the second line for the second section, and the final note of hope for the third section. After praying Psalm 42–43 in this way you will be better able to see a connection with the scene in the garden of Gethsemane and better prepared to enter into the prayer of Jesus' lament.

Jesus' Prayer in Gethsemane

Many biblical commentators today believe that Psalm 42–43 with its common refrain and mood of lament has influenced the gospel accounts of Jesus at prayer in Gethsemane. The passion narratives appear to be the unique place in the New Testament where this form of prayer is recalled or exhibited by an individual at prayer. In this gospel scene, Jesus appears fearful in the face of death. Despite this fear, he exhibits a sense of support from his faith in God. In Matthew's portrayal of Jesus' prayer in Gethsemane we hear an echo of Psalm 42–43. It is an eloquent expression of the ancient psalmist's longing for God while in the midst of intense suffering and the fear of impending death. The blending of this psalm with Matthew's scene of Jesus' praying in the garden presents us with new motives for honesty in prayer. They challenge us to bring our true selves before the Lord after the example of Jesus who prayed in the mood of a lament while in Gethsemane. Matthew clearly intends this prayer to be a model for our own prayer since Jesus instructs his disciples to remain with him in the garden, to watch and to pray (Matt 26:38, 41). With this in mind, we enter honestly into prayerful reflection with both texts influencing our thoughts.

THE PSALM: "WHY ARE YOU CAST DOWN, O MY SOUL?"
(Ps 42:5a)

In the first section of the psalm the person at prayer bemoans his or her state of soul, yet prays out of an intense longing for God. This longing is increased by the memory of participation in past Jewish festivals, especially worship in the Temple with lavish processions. This memory is the basis for a new hope, for God who called and cradles the people of Israel is a faithful God and present to the most distraught soul. So why be downcast? Feelings are one thing, but faith in the living God is quite another. Resist the taunters' cry, "Where is your God?" (Ps 42:3) and the temptation to doubt. You know where God is. God is with you, just as God is always with Israel.

THE GARDEN: "I AM DEEPLY GRIEVED, EVEN TO DEATH"
(Matt 26:38a)

This verse echoes the plaintive cry of the psalmist, "Why are you cast down, O my soul?" (Ps 42:5, 11; 43:5). Jesus' soul appears downcast, heaviness fills his heart. Yet he is not without hope. He approaches the moment of his impending passion primed for prayer. He and his disciples have just celebrated the Passover meal. This Passover was unique. It was Jesus' last meal with those he loved and called to follow him. Undoubtedly the moment was filled with unspeakable sadness. Yet, it was still the Passover, filled with the richness of memory and boundless joy in the saving power of the God of Israel.

As Jesus and his disciples finish their meal, Matthew says, "when they had sung the hymn, they went out to the Mount of Olives" (26:30). This verse is pivotal for entering into the transition from the supper and its psalms of praise to the garden and the intense prayer of Jesus' lament. Among the hymns of the Passover were the praise psalms (114–118), which celebrate God's gracious deliverance of Israel from Egypt. Jesus therefore began to approach his God in deep personal prayer with the strains of Israel's public praise still echoing in his heart: "I was pushed hard so that I was falling . . . , The Lord is my strength and my might . . . , I shall not die but I shall live." (Ps 118:13, 14, 17). Thus Jesus proceeds from table prayer to garden lament with an inner awareness of the comforting presence of the God of Israel being with him.

THE PSALM: "WHY ARE YOU DISQUIETED WITHIN ME?"
(Ps 42:11b)

Again the taunters tempt the prayerful psalmist to doubt. "Where is your God?" they cry. As this doubtfulness passes over the inner spirit of the person at prayer, the psalmist remembers God and the beauty of the northern mountains with the cascading waters that form the Jordan River. Just as this abundant water is ever present, so God's steadfast love is present day after day, giving rise to the psalmist's prayer at night. The feeling of death may be in the bones of the one praying, but a song to God the "rock" is in the heart (Ps 42:8, 9a, 10).

THE GARDEN: "STAY AWAKE AND PRAY" (Matt 26:41a)

Unlike the Gospel of Mark, which emphasizes the sleepiness of the disciples, Matthew highlights three distinct periods of Jesus' prayer in the garden. Jesus invites his disciples to watch and pray with him. Keeping watch with the Lord will instruct them how to pray as Jesus prays. This is something Jesus has done before in the Gospel of Matthew (Matt 6:5-13; 11:25-30). Despite his present sorrow, his mood does not cloud his faith-vision. He goes prayerfully before his God in a posture of deep reverence, his body prostrate upon the ground.

Echo of an Earlier Prayer

Jesus' garden prayer speaks of his profound relationship with his God. He prays as a son to the God he calls "My Father" (26:39, 42). Even though he pleads for the Father to remove the cup of his suffering, Jesus echoes the deep and trusting sentiments of the prayer he has already taught to his disciples: "Your will be done" (6:10b). Jesus' prayer in Gethsemane gives witness that he prays as the righteous one who accomplishes God's will. He lives his own teaching on prayer. He does not pray to be seen (6:5-6), he does not heap up empty words (6:7-8); Jesus prays as he has instructed his disciples, to seek God's kingdom and God's will (6:9-13). On the lips of Jesus, the words "My Father" are not a repetitious or an empty prayer, they are an affirmation of a deep commitment based on a union of heart and will.

In the second period of prayer, Jesus' heart moves to a new level of union and acceptance. The cup he prayed might pass from his lips, he is now willing to accept. Jesus has said he would not drink of the cup until he would drink new wine in the kingdom of his Father (26:29). Now having drunk of the cup of the covenant at the supper, Jesus is ready to consume the cup of his sufferings, in order to usher in the coming kingdom according to the will of his Father (26:42). Like the psalmist who prayed long before him, Jesus now prays his song of faithfulness, not with shouts of exultation, but with deep sighs of inner acceptance.

Jesus' prayer is one of profound agony and darkest night. It is a prayer in which the disciples are invited to share. It is, however, not a prayer without hope. Ultimately Jesus' prayer is geared not only to fortify him for his passion, but also to engage him in the work of revealing the Father's kingdom. In that kingdom, Jesus will once again share the cup of new life with his disciples.

THE PSALM: "HOPE IN GOD!
FOR I SHALL AGAIN PRAISE HIM . . . " (Ps 43:5c)

The psalmist has looked to the past, and in the memory of God's abiding love has found a new and present strength. Though saddened in spirit, through memory-celebration the one praying knows that no one is ever separated from the mighty works of God. God's saving deeds are real and ever-present. Despite a downcast spirit, rather than collapse into the shifting sands of human emotion, the psalmist is willing to build a renewed hope on the solid foundation of God's faithfulness. A powerful lesson indeed!

Just as God once called and delivered the people of Israel, leading them with a pillar of cloud and fire, now the psalmist calls upon the Lord to vindicate and to lead with God's own fidelity and light as a guide once again (Ps 43:1, 3). This form of direct prayer appeal personifies God's care and guidance. God is the faithful light who once led the people out of darkness. Now this same God will lead the person praying out of this present state of darkness of soul into the light of a new day. Exodus is not just an event of past deliverance; Exodus is an ever-present experience for those who reverently approach the Lord with a faithful spirit and a hopeful heart.

THE GARDEN: "SEE, THE HOUR IS AT HAND" (Matt 26:45b)

Jesus' three-fold prayer emphasizes his commitment to and perseverance in prayer. It also demonstrates his willingness to accept the cup of suffering not only in his devotion but through his adherence to the Father's will. It is a struggle to accept, but accept it he does. Matthew emphasizes this struggle and acceptance by having Jesus go before God in prayer a third time repeating the words of his previous prayer, "My Father, if this cannot pass unless I drink it, your will be done" (26:42, 44).

With this prayer of acceptance not only on his lips, but firmly rooted in his soul, Jesus is now ready to face his Exodus-hour. Because God's light and fidelity will lead him, Jesus has a measure of hope. It is not a frivolous hope, the mood is too somber for that. It is a stable hope built on the self-assurance that only comes from total trust in God. Thus Jesus can say to his disciples, "Get up, let us be going. Look, my betrayer is at hand" (26:46).

Fulfillment in Prayer

The words of Jesus are about to be fulfilled: "You will all become deserters because of me this night" (26:31). This night is the hour of the "striking of the shepherd," yet it is not a night without a glimmer of hope both for the shepherd and the sheep. Had not Jesus said, "After I am raised up I will go ahead of you to Galilee" (26:31-32)? Despite the present moment of sleepiness and their failure in the test of watchfulness, the disciples will one day awaken to the experience of Jesus' Exodus-resurrection. Like the psalmist before them, they too will go up to the "land of Jordan and of Hermon," to Galilee, and there remember their Savior and their God once again, their hearts filled with new hope and new life. (Ps 42:6; 43:5c). How many times in our own prayer does God call us to transcend our mood or our feelings so that we might enter into the land of God's hope once again. Lament is balanced with praise. Yes, "Hope in God; for I shall again praise him . . . " (Ps 43:5c).

Prayer Exercises

From Table to Garden (26:30; 26:36-46)

In a short space of time the prayer mood of Jesus shifts a great deal.

- At the Passover table Jesus and his disciples prayed psalms of praise designated for the paschal feast. Read Psalms 115, 116, and 117 to savor some of their mood.
- In the garden Jesus prays alone, his mood quickly shifting to dread-filled thoughts of his impending passion. This form of prayer is called a lament. Read Psalms 22 and 130 to experience their prayerful cry to God.
- Reflect upon your own changes of mood in prayer. What causes these changes? Do you respond equally in prayer to moments of joy, as in moments of sorrow or fear? What prayer response do you make in each circumstance?

Prayer to God (6:5-15)

Like Jesus we often pray the "Lord's Prayer" to God as parent. Have we really made it our own prayer, expressive of a real bond with God? The proof of this bond may be found in our own prayers of trial and lament. Think of something that troubles you and pray about it. Are you able to persevere in that prayer? Are you able to face both fact and feelings as you talk to God about your dilemma?

Agonizing Prayer to God (26:36-46)

Like Jesus we are called to face trial and darkness, temptation and despair, even death. Think of the most difficult challenge in your life thus far. Can you go back and ask Jesus to be with you as you face your unresolved feelings about whatever it was that challenged you? Use Psalm 42–43 as a guide in your prayer. As you face the challenge, remember the blessings of your life as well. Recall the words of the psalmist: "Hope in God; for I shall again praise him . . . " (Ps 42:5, 11; 43:5).

Recommended Reading

Anderson, A. *Commentary on the Psalms.* 2 vols. New Century Bible Commentary. Grand Rapids, Mich.: William B. Eerdmans, 1981.

Brueggemann, Walter. *Praying the Psalms.* Winona, Minn.: St. Mary's Press, 1986.

Harrington, Daniel J., S.J. *The Gospel According to Matthew.* Collegeville, Minn.: The Liturgical Press, 1983.

_____. *The Gospel of Matthew,* Sacra Pagina Series, vol. 1. Collegeville, Minn.: The Liturgical Press, A Michael Glazier Book, 1991.

Matera, Frank. *Passion Narratives and Gospel Theologies.* New York: Paulist Press, 1986.

Meier, John, S.J. *Matthew.* Wilmington, Del.: Michael Glazier, 1981.

Miller, P. "Trouble and Woe." *Interpretation* 37 (January 1983) 32–45.

Senior, Donald, C.P. *The Passion of Jesus in the Gospel of Matthew.* Wilmington, Del.: Michael Glazier, 1984.

Stanley, David, S.J. *Jesus in Gethsemane.* New York: Paulist Press, 1980.

Stuhlmueller, Carroll, C.P. *Psalms.* 2 vols. Wilmington, Del.: Michael Glazier, 1983.

Trocmé, Etienne. *The Passion as Liturgy.* London: SCM Press, 1983.

Chapter 4

"On the Way"
Luke's Challenge to
Compassionate Gospel Living

The story of the two disciples' journey and encounter with the crucified and risen Christ on the road to Emmaus is a wonderful section of Scripture for prayer and reflection. Each prayerful reading reveals new dimensions of this fascinating story. Luke, a master storyteller, weaves this unique account of the resurrection event into the fabric of his already creative telling of the life and ministry of Jesus. For Luke, Jesus is always on the road, moving toward his destiny in Jerusalem (9:51; 13:22; 17:11; 19:28, 41, 45).

The Road to Emmaus (24:13-35)

In this story of two bewildered disciples, Luke holds up a mirror in which we can see not only the gospel story reflected, but also our own call to a more committed dis-

cipleship. How wonderfully Luke draws us into the story
as we join the two disciples in their discussion of the events
of the previous three days. Aware that the One who accom-
panies them on their journey is the risen Christ, we listen
even more intently as they recall their memories of Jesus,
"a prophet mighty in deed and word before God and all
the people" (24:19). After hearing their tale, the risen Christ
reflects with them on the meaning of his life and ministry.
The message of this wordy walk is that the Messiah had to
suffer these things in order to enter into his glory (24:26).

The Journey Foreshadowed

In the early part of his Gospel Luke presents Jesus as
a teacher and healer similar to the portrayals of Mark and
Matthew. One feature that makes Luke's portrayal of the
life and ministry of Jesus a bit different is the central section of his Gospel, known as the journey narrative (9:51–
19:28). Immediately preceding this story of Jesus' journey
to Jerusalem, Luke presents two predictions of the passion
and death of Jesus and the event we call the Transfiguration.

Transfiguration of the Journey (9:28-38)

For Luke, Jesus is a man of prayer. Over and over again
Jesus is portrayed as a person who is intimately linked with
God in prayer (9:18, 28; 10:21; 11:1). This bond is his
strength, giving him the courage not only to pursue the journey himself, but to invite others to travel with him in faithful discipleship. The two motifs are linked for Luke—
Christ's passion and the Christian pilgrimage go together.

Immediately following Peter's confession that Jesus is
the Messiah (9:20), Jesus instructs his disciples about his
forthcoming passion in Jerusalem. He then invites them to
become his followers and to make the journey with him.
Jesus' statement that "The Son of Man must undergo great
suffering . . . and be killed, and on the third day be raised"
(9:22) is immediately followed by "If any want to become

my followers, let them . . . take up their cross daily and
follow me" (9:23). To follow Jesus is to walk the journey
with him. This is the message to the pilgrims on the Emmaus road after the resurrection. This is also the message
to the reader-disciple as the gospel journey unfolds in Luke's
narrative.

Just as the Emmaus story is a mirror reflecting the
events of Christ's life, death, and resurrection, the event
of the Transfiguration as told by Luke acts as a reflective
lens through which we preview the journey and destiny of
Jesus. It is a transforming moment for Jesus as well. There
on the mountain Jesus' face, clothing, his entire destiny are
transformed in dazzling glory. It is a prayerful encounter
with God in which Jesus glimpses his exodus and future
glory. The reader joins him not only in prayer on the mountain, but at the beginning of his journey to Jerusalem
(9:28-36). All who see and hear this event are invited not
merely to "Listen to him" (9:35) but also to follow him.
This Jesus is God's Chosen One, who, because of this transforming experience, is now firmly resolved to proceed toward Jerusalem (9:51), and who invites all who share the
same vision to "Follow me" (9:59).

The Journey Enacted

As the journey is about to commence, the reader may
well recall the first steps of Jesus' ministry recorded by Luke.
Jesus began his ministry steeped in Israel's prayer, its synagogue service of word and reflection. There he read the
prophetic words, "The Spirit of the Lord is upon me"; God
"has sent me to proclaim release to the captives and recov-
ery of sight to the blind, to let the oppressed go free" (4:18).
Modeling his ministry after the prophet Elijah who reached
out to a widowed foreigner, Jesus began his journey reaching out to and including the outcasts and public sinners of
his day. Throughout Luke's Gospel Jesus embodies the journey motif of Moses and the ministry of Elijah. Their com-

bined appearance to him on the mountain signal a new phase in his movement toward Jerusalem (9:30-31). With one sweeping sentence Luke begins the ascent not only to Jerusalem, but to glory. "When the days drew near for him to be taken up, he set his face to go to Jerusalem" (9:51).

As the journey to Jerusalem begins Jesus sends out his band of disciples two by two for their first taste of gospel ministry. "Go on your way," Jesus instructs them, and remember, "Whoever listens to you listens to me" (10:3; 16). Pairs of disciples will also be remembered at the arrival in Jerusalem and in the passion narrative as they proceed in twos once again to prepare the way for Jesus' arrival in the city, prepare the table for his last meal with the disciples, and prepare the way for others to meet him on their own journey of life (10:1; 19:29-30; 23:8; 24:13-15). For now they are a simple reminder that we are invited to walk with Jesus seeing and hearing his ministry and message in a spirit of joy. Three times joy is mentioned in a few short lines. The disciples return rejoicing in their experience, Jesus rejoices in the Spirit and offers joyful praise to God for the disciples' success. Despite all obstacles, even persecution, our gospel mission and message is meant to be one of joy (10:17, 20, 21).

The message of joy becomes clearer in the ministry of Jesus, especially in his teaching. Throughout the narrative of Jesus' journey toward Jerusalem, Luke portrays Jesus as the bearer of good news. This is evident in three parables that are found only in the Gospel of Luke: the Good Samaritan, the prodigal son, and the rich man and the poor Lazarus.

From Outcasts to Ministers

THE GOOD SAMARITAN (10:25-37)

In this brief but beautiful story we are challenged to answer the question, "Who is my neighbor?" (10:29). Like the lawyer we are aware of the great commandments to love God and our neighbor, yet as we walk the journey of life are we really ready and willing to help those in need, those beaten and battered and left alone by the roadside of life? Or do we pass them by like the professionally religious people, the priest and Levite, of Jesus' story? As Jesus weaves this story, it is the outcast Samaritan who stuns us. He alone halts his journey to let pity move his heart and help the one in need. The compassion of this unlikely stranger forces us to ask some difficult questions. Are we too busy, too hard-hearted, or too uncaring to reach out to others whose need arises on the path of our journey? Isn't that the test, to be willing to pause in our own journey to assist someone in theirs? That is the test of faithful discipleship, because it is the test of love.

This test on the Jericho road is the test of the journey of life because it is at the heart of the gospel message, the message of compassion and concern. Later in Luke's Gospel, Jesus himself will embody this message as he pauses to minister to Zacchaeus on the same Jericho road. For now we pause to reflect on the ministry of a lowly Samaritan to a fellow traveler in need and to listen to the challenging word of Jesus: "Go and do likewise" (10:37).

THE WAYWARD OR PRODIGAL SON (15:1-32)

As Jesus' journey progresses he moves toward Jerusalem. Eating and drinking what is put before him, he dines in the homes of friends and Pharisees alike (10:30; 14:1). In all of these events Jesus invites others to heed his message and to follow his example of ministry to sinners and outcasts. He even shared table-fellowship with them, prompting his accusers to say, "This fellow welcomes sinners and eats with them" (15:2).

In three specifically Lucan parables Jesus invites his followers to enter into the heart of his ministry and outreach to sinners. Through the voices of a shepherd who retrieves a single lost sheep, a woman who recovers a single lost coin, and a father who reconciles a wayward lost son, we are urged to explore the meaning of the gospel message and invitation: "Rejoice with me" (15:6, 9, 32). The shepherd, the woman, and the father all echo God's voice speaking through Jesus as he calls sinners and outcasts to the joyful banquet of God's kingdom.

This ministry of Jesus to outcasts and sinners is a scandal to the religious leaders of Israel. Like those rigid leaders, the slavishly loyal other son of the forgiving father can't heed the message of Jesus' story. Thus God's loving embrace, God's lavish mercy, God's kingdom banquet is rejected because a "loyal" son won't let his father embody the gospel message of mercy and forgiveness. "This brother of yours was dead and has come to life; he was lost and has been found, . . . we had to celebrate and rejoice!" (15:32). In this final scene of the moving parable the wayward but now reconciled son silently joins his father in pleading with his brother to join in the banquet of God's mercy and forgiveness. The real journey is to move from being an outcast to being a minister at the rich banquet of God's kingdom. To sit at table with Jesus is to share in the ministry of God's reconciling love. The constant message of Luke's Gospel is that in Jesus we have met someone who welcomes sinners and will share a meal with them. This is truly reason to rejoice.

THE POOR BEGGAR (16:19-31)

The journey and teaching of Jesus continue, this time turning to the poor. In the parable of the rich man who dines sumptuously each day, Lazarus is a poor man who begs for scraps of food at the rich man's table. Eventually both men die. Lazarus is raised to the heavenly banquet described as the bosom of Abraham, and the rich man moans in torment from the abode of the dead. From there he cries out, "Father Abraham, have mercy on me" (16:24). Abraham reminds him that he has had his reward, and now a great abyss separates him from life and consolation. It is too late to cross over the boundaries now. The attitudes that separated him from Lazarus and the plight of the poor in life now separate him from the peace of the kingdom in the afterlife. Now it is too late, even Father Abraham cannot invite the rich man to the banquet table of the kingdom.

"What about my brothers who are still living?" the tormented man inquires. "Send Lazarus to be a warning to them." "They have Moses and the prophets, they should listen to them," Abraham replies. "If they do not listen to Moses and the prophets, neither will they be convinced even if someone rises from the dead" (16:29-31). It seems even the message of the Risen One can go unheeded if we are not willing to see him as the embodiment of Moses' journey and Elijah's ministry. Luke's constant message is that in his journey to Jerusalem Jesus is constantly reaching out to the poor, sinners, the very outcasts of society. He does this in a way that proclaims the inaugural message of the Lord's anointed servant who in the person of Jesus mirrors the deeds and echoes the voices of the compassionate Samaritan, the lost son, and the poor Lazarus, who all announce the joyful message of the in-breaking kingdom of God's mercy (4:18).

The Journey Fulfilled

The journey is about to reach its destination— Jerusalem, slayer of the prophets. Jesus himself has said, "I must be on my way, because it is impossible for a prophet to be killed outside of Jerusalem" (13:33). Now on the threshold of the city, Jesus walks the Jericho road soon to be beaten and robbed of his own life. "See we are going up to Jerusalem and everything that is written . . . by the prophets will be accomplished. After they have flogged him, they will kill him, and on the third day he will rise again" (18:31, 33).

THE ROAD TO JERICHO (19:1-10)

With the third and last prediction of the passion still ringing in our ears, Jesus enters the city of Jericho. There a man named Zacchaeus looks down from the branches of a sycamore tree he has climbed. From that perch, he is trying to see what Jesus is like (19:3). Zacchaeus was small in stature, yet important by position. He was a chief tax collector and a wealthy person, reasons enough to be despised by the citizens of Jericho. They see him as an outsider. No wonder Jesus is attracted to him.

Like the searching shepherd and the house-cleaning woman Jesus retrieves the lost Zacchaeus and brings him to his own home rejoicing in God's kingdom while all his "elder brothers" shake their fingers in bewilderment saying, "He has gone to be the guest of one who is a sinner," while growing in their awareness that "Today salvation has come to this house" (19:7, 9). Like the elder brother of the wayward and prodigal son the grumbling crowd refuses to accept the saving mission of Jesus. Meanwhile, like those reclaimed in the parables before this event, Zacchaeus rejoices in the table fellowship of the kingdom. His home and his table become the healing refuge of the innkeeper's lodging, the festal surroundings of the prodigal's homestead, and the life-giving haven of the bosom of Abraham. In the company of Jesus, parables become reality—stories of salvation become kingdom moments in the journey of life helping us to see what Jesus is really like.

THE ROAD TO CALVARY (23:26-43)

The pace of Luke's journey narrative quickens and soon Jesus is in Jerusalem (19:28, 41, 45). The action moves rapidly from his final teaching in the Temple to last table fellowship with his disciples. Arrest and trial follow quickly and soon we join the condemned Jesus in the final stage of his journey, the way of the Cross. In two short scenes

Luke summarizes much of his message about the meaning of Jesus' ministry.

In the mini-journey we call the way of the Cross, Jesus walks the last few steps in the journey of his life. Walking behind him, just as Jesus said his disciples would do, Simon of Cyrene carries the cross (9:23). Faithful discipleship is a call to journey with Jesus to the very end (23:26).

Two others also accompany Jesus along the way. These, however, are far from images of faithfulness. They are criminals and outcasts—images of those to whom Jesus has continuously offered salvation throughout his preaching and ministry along the journey to Jerusalem. Jesus had often eaten with sinners, now he will die with them. Luke's message is constant; what Jesus had preached at the tables of God's inbreaking Kingdom he now proclaims from the tree of the cross: "Father, forgive them" (23:24). Mercy's dying breath is a plea for mercy, the gift of God's salvation is found not in some distant dining hall, but here at the cross, today. What the searching Zacchaeus glimpsed from the sycamore tree and knew in his home in Jericho, a repentant criminal now knows in his heart as he gazes at Jesus from the branches of his cross. Seeing what Jesus is like, he makes the simple request, "Jesus, remember me," and is rewarded with "Paradise," a symbol of God's lavish and eternal banquet given in the kingdom, this very day (23:42, 43).

BACK ON THE EMMAUS ROAD (24:13-35)

In the final scenes of his Gospel, Luke resumes his journey motif. Throughout the Gospel the movement was toward Jerusalem; now it is just the reverse. Jesus invited his followers to accompany him to Jerusalem, the place of his passion and glory, now the disciples walk away confused and dejected. However, Jesus still walks with them. This is the genius of Luke's Emmaus story. Companionship with Jesus is still available to those who have eyes to see and ears to hear (9:23, 24). Once again it is the moment of table fellowship that reveals the saving presence of Jesus, now the Risen One but still in the company of his disciples.

Two by two the disciples discover him in their midst once again. "Were not our hearts burning within us while he was talking to us on the road?" They had also come to know him at table in the breaking of the bread (24:32, 35). Now not only eyes but hearts are opened to the meaning of the Scriptures. What were predictions of the passion (9:22, 44; 18:31-33) are now revelations of his risen presence. "Was it not necessary that the Messiah should suffer these things and then enter into his glory?" (24:26). What began on a mountaintop with Moses and Elijah is now transfigured once again. "Beginning with Moses and the prophets, he interpreted to them the things about himself in all the scriptures" (24:27).

Journey in Prayer

The road to Emmaus becomes the road to Jerusalem once more. Turned around by the saving presence of Christ, the disciples go up to Jerusalem once again. Once there they will hear the Risen One say, "Thus it is written, that the Messiah is to suffer and rise from the dead on the third day, and that repentance and forgiveness of sins is to be proclaimed in his name to all the nations beginning from Jerusalem" (24:46, 47). There in the Jerusalem of our hearts, a new journey and a new challenge is about to begin.

Prayer Exercises

Emmaus Journey (24:13-35)

Emmaus is a journey backward to help you go forward. If you reflect on your own journey with Jesus in life thus far, what events of your personal story will help you to continue on the journey? How was Christ present at critical moments of that journey? What word did he speak or insight did he give to help you go on?

Transfiguration (9:28-36)

As Moses and Elijah were for Jesus, you also have guides along the journey of life, mentors, to show forth and interpret the way. Who are these mentors for you? Have you remained faithful to the path they have shown? Pray about these guides in your life and your faithfulness to them.

The Good Samaritan (10:25-37)

What is the more important question for you, "How do I read the law?" or "Who is my neighbor?" What response would best help you comply with Jesus' injunction, "Go and do likewise"?

The Wayward or Prodigal Son (15:11-32)

With what person in the story do you most identify: the wayward son? the forgiving father? the unaccepting brother? As you identify with one of the characters, how do you feel about the other two persons? What do you say to them? What do you pray for them?

The Rich Man and the Poor Beggar (16:19-31)

This is a judgment story. If you were to die today how would God judge you? Remember Jesus is again saying, "Blessed . . . are those who hear the word of God and obey it" (11:28). Where is the voice of the Risen One for you? He is your judge, now and hereafter; what is his message to you? Pray about this in the light of Jesus' saying in 9:23-26.

Roads to Walk

Prayerfully choose to walk down one of these roads:

The road to Jericho　(18:35-43)
　　　　　　　　　　(19:1-10)
The road to Calvary　(23:26-56)
The road to Emmaus (24:13-35)

Whom do you see? With whom do you want to stop and talk? What do you say? What do you need from them to keep on going? What is your prayer for yourself as you resume your journey?

Recommended Reading

Johnson, Luke T., *The Gospel of Luke,* Sacra Pagina Series, vol. 3. Collegeville, Minn.: The Liturgical Press, A Michael Glazier Book, 1991.

Karris, Robert J., O.F.M. *Luke, Artist and Theologian.* Mahwah, N.J.: Paulist Press, 1985.

Kodell, Jerome, O.S.B. *The Gospel According to Luke.* Collegeville, Minn.: The Liturgical Press, 1983.

Laverdiere, Eugene, S.S.S. *Luke.* Wilmington, Del.: Michael Glazier, 1980.

_____. ''The Passion-Ressurrection of Jesus According to Luke.'' *Chicago Studies* 25 (April 1986) 35–50.

Matera, Frank. *Passion Narratives and Gospel Theologies.* New York: Paulist Press, 1986.

Moessner, David P. *Lord of the Banquet: Literary and Theological Significance of the Lucan Travel Narrative.* Minneapolis, Minn.: Augsburg Fortress, 1989.

Senior, Donald, C.P. *The Passion of Jesus in the Gospel of Luke.* Wilmington, Del.: Michael Glazier, 1989.

Sweetland, Dennis, M. *Our Journey with Jesus: Discipleship According to Luke-Acts.* Collegeville, Minn.: The Liturgical Press, A Michael Glazier Book, 1990.

Van Linden, Philip, C.M. *The Gospel of Luke and Acts.* Wilmington, Del.: Michael Glazier, 1986.

Chapter 5

"By the Cross"
John's Portrait of
Jesus, the Paschal Lamb

From the earliest gatherings of Christian faithful the story of Jesus' dying and rising has been the object of prayerful reflection and community celebration (cf. Acts 2:42; 3:18; 1 Cor 11:26). Just as the Hebrew Passover focused on the retelling of the Exodus event, early Christians began to narrate the story of their Lord's death and resurrection. This story was not told simply as an historical event. Rather, from the very beginning, it was narrated and interpreted using the language and images of the Hebrew Scriptures.

The Gospel of John is well known for its signs and images which have been the subject of many reflections and the object of much prayer down through the ages of Christian thought and devotion. Once again these signs and images provide a focus for a new and prayerful reflection on the death of Jesus in the passion narrative in John's Gospel.

By the time John's Gospel was written the awareness of Jesus' death and resurrection as a saving act of God was deeply embedded in Christian experience. This was most evident in Christian prayer and liturgical celebration. John's narrative of his Lord's death reads more like a meditation on the passion, taking as its starting-point the traditional story, but seeking not so much to retell it as to interpret it. In this way John spells out the deeper religious truths implied in the events of that fateful day when the Son of God was crucified.

The idea that John's passion narrative is as much a meditation as a narrative is intriguing. John's use of sign and image influence his writing so directly. In many ways as John tells his story of Jesus' dying and rising, he does so not only by telling us about one who suffers at the hands of others, but one who orchestrates these events until the climactic moment of his final self-revelation. This self-revelation seems to be directly connected with the image of the Hebrew Passover and the Johannine insight that Jesus is the "Lamb of God" (1:29).

A Passover Motif

John mentions the Hebrew Passover at the beginning of his account of Jesus' final days, indeed his final "hour." In one sweeping sentence John begins the second half of his Gospel, the "Book of Glory": "Now before the festival of the Passover, Jesus knew that his hour had come to depart from this world and to go to the Father" (13:1). By citing the approach of Passover, John signals his reader that he understands his passion narrative to be a Passover story. The phrase, "The Passover of the Jews was near," occurs throughout the Gospel narrative, almost like a refrain.

References to Passover occur at key moments in the prelude of events that lead up to John's dramatic portrayal of the death of Jesus (2:13; 6:4; 11:55). The events surrounding the purification of the Temple, the discourse on the bread of life, and the raising of Lazarus all prompt the reader to focus on Jesus. For, when his "hour" is at hand, as the final celebration of the feast of Passover approaches, Jesus will be revealed in John's Gospel as the sign that replaces the Temple, the bread whose flesh is given for life of the world, and the glorified and risen presence of life itself.

John's Replacement Theme

The continued references to the Passover help to weave a narrative that invites the reader to reflect on the paschal significance of Jesus himself. The first reference to the Passover occurs after the sign at Cana where Jesus provides an abundance of wine for the wedding guests. The second Passover reference is at the time of the feeding of the multitudes when Jesus provides an abundance of bread for the weary pilgrims who follow him. These two Passover signs are transformed in the "Book of Glory" where John portrays Jesus as the sign of God's abundant love in the self gift of laying down his life for others (13:3-5; 15:13).

According to John, Jesus was crucified on the eve of the feast of Unleavened Bread, the Passover (18:28; 19:14, 31), at the very hour the lambs for the feast were being slaughtered in the Temple. In John's view, Jesus is the replacement for these lambs, thus giving the feast a new and Christian meaning. This image mirrors John's earlier statement that Jesus is the true "Lamb of God" (John 1:29). It is reflected in both the prophecy of Isaiah (Isa 53:7) and in the description of the Passover in the Book of Exodus (Exod 12:5). These dual images merge in the passion narrative of John's Gospel through his use of key verses from the psalms, chosen to invite the reader to ponder the truth that Jesus died in accordance with the Scriptures (19:24, 28, 36).

Praying the Psalms at the Foot of the Cross

The scene of Jesus' crucifixion and death in John's Gospel includes a number of highly charged events that are unique to his account of the passion. Especially noteworthy are the events of the casting of lots for Jesus' seamless garment (19:23-24), the thirst of Jesus (19:28-30), and the keeping of Jesus' body intact while the legs of the others crucified with him are broken (19:31-33). What is also unique to John is that all of these events are recorded, "so that the scriptures might be fulfilled" (19:24, 28, 36).

John cites the passages fulfilled for two of these events. In all three cases, the scriptural passages are either from psalm verses describing the afflictions of the innocent Servant of Israel or from passages related to the ceremonies surrounding the Passover lamb. Meditative reflection on these key psalm texts provide rich insight into John's image of Jesus as the Lamb of God.

"THEY DIVIDE MY GARMENTS" (19:23-25)

"They divided my clothes among themselves, and for my clothing they cast lots" (Ps 22:18). Psalm 22 is important in all the passion narratives. Matthew and Mark quote Jesus crying out with the opening verse of the psalm (Ps 22:1) and Luke mentions the mockery of the crowd as an echo of the accusers lashing out unjustly at the Servant of Israel (Ps 22:7-8) (see Matt 27:39; Mark 15:29; Luke 23:35-36). Only John uses Psalm 22 in reference to the dividing and casting of lots for Jesus' garments.

John portrays the poetic parallelism of Psalm 22:18 as two actions in his narrative. The soldiers take Jesus' clothes, his outer garments, and divide them into four shares, one for each soldier. Jesus' undergarment, the tunic, "was seamless woven in one piece from the top" (John 19:23) so rather than tear it, the soldiers cast lots to keep it intact.

A tunic was a long ankle-length garment worn over the body. It was woven in one piece and had no seam. Such a garment is described as the vesture of the high priest in Exodus 28:4; 39:27 and in Leviticus 16:4. The prescriptions

of Leviticus forbid the high priest from tearing his garments
(Lev 21:10).

The fact that Jesus' tunic was without seam is a tan-
talizing detail. By highlighting this fact John seems to draw
our attention to a possible priestly symbolism. The real significance lies, however, in John's usage of Psalm 22. Though
his choice of verse 18 is unique, by using the psalm in his
narrative John gives evidence to the fact that this psalm was
traditionally employed by the early Church as a way of
meditating and reflecting on the crucifixion of Christ.

Psalm 22 describes the sufferings of the Just One, the
Servant of Israel. Surrounded by enemies, the servant cries
out for deliverance from God. John uses Psalm 22 to demon-
strate that Jesus' death is not an accident, but a part of God's
saving plan. Instead of having Jesus cry out in apparent
abandonment, John utilizes Psalm 22 to develop his theme
that Jesus died in accord with the Scriptures. He does so
by making a symbolic allusion to Jesus as high priest.

While this priestly reference is symbolic, the psalm itself is most certainly the lament of someone who is suffering. It is an eloquent cry to God to hear the prayer of the
one in torment. Most likely this prayer was the result of a
prolonged ordeal. Yet the one praying moves from a state
of desperate outcry in which God does not seem to answer
the petitioner (Ps 22:2) to a transitional moment of recog-
nition when God hears and draws near to help in time of
affliction (Ps 22:19-21). "My God, I cry out by day, but
you do not answer; and by night, but find no rest" (Ps 22:2).
"In you our ancestors trusted, they trusted and you delivered them. To you they cried and were saved" (Ps 22:4, 5).
"But you, O Lord, do not be far away, O my help, come
quickly to my aid. Deliver my soul . . . save me" (Ps 22:19,
20, 21).

Because this personal lament is so vivid, it became part
of the fabric of Israel's communal worship, expressing the
timeless praise of her ever-faithful God. Israel's conscious-

ness surrounding this psalm developed to such a degree that a pious Jew like Jesus who pondered the Scriptures, especially the Servant Songs of Isaiah, could instinctively pray this prayer as an expression of his awareness of God's care in the hour of personal need.

John's reflection on Jesus' embodiment of this psalm at the cross is a unique meditation on the passion as an experience of Israel's Suffering Servant now manifest in the unjustly crucified Jesus. It may even be an expression of the collective unconsciousness of Israel's awareness of God's constant and ever-present care. Jesus may not have so much fulfilled the words of this Hebrew prayer in the agony of his passion, as he may have given reason to a person like John to meditate on the deeper meanings revealed in the passion event through a prayerful and unique reflection on this psalm.

"I THIRST" (19:28-30)

The Johannine scene of Jesus' death is marked by symbol and simplicity. Jesus dies almost presiding over the events of his own passing. He proclaims, "It is finished," in a quiet but confident manner (19:30). Meditating along with the Gospel writer we begin to see a deeper meaning in the finality of Jesus' death.

John presents the death scene in terms of the absolute finality surrounding Jesus' dying. His death is his greatest work. In his dying breath Jesus proclaims his awareness that his work is done, everything is now finished (19:30). In the beginning of the "Book of Glory," John states: "Now before the festival of the Passover, Jesus knew his hour had come to depart from this world and go to the Father. Having loved his own who were in the world, he loved them to the end" (13:1). For John the word *end* is filled with deep significance. It denotes not only completion but absolute finality. By his focus on the finality of Jesus' death on the cross, the evangelist draws the reader into a meditation on the ultimate expression of God's work accomplished in Jesus. In the death of Jesus God has embraced the world with the ultimate finality of Love's embrace. In Jesus' dying breath, God's work is totally accomplished (see 3:16).

Earlier in John's Gospel Jesus has spoken of the work he will accomplish. It is the work of his Father who has sent him. This work and its accomplishment is nourishment for Jesus. "My food," Jesus says, "is to do the will of him who sent me and to complete his work" (4:34). In his great prayer at table with "his own" Jesus prays, "I glorified you on earth by finishing the work that you gave me to do" (17:4). Now that his hour has come and the end is near, Jesus is about to drink the cup of his sufferings and complete the work he came to do, all in fulfillment of the Scriptures.

Throughout John's Gospel Jesus hungers and thirsts for the Father's will to be accomplished (4:34; 18:11). In John, hunger and thirst are image words for the desire of Jesus to fulfill the will of his father to the very end. At the time of the arrest in the garden, Jesus responded to Peter's attempt to defend him, "Put your sword back into its sheath. Am I not to drink the cup that the Father has given me?" (18:11) In contrast to the Synoptic Gospels where Jesus prayed that the cup be removed from him (cf. Matt 26:39; Mark 14:36; Luke 22:43), the Johannine Jesus wants no obstacle put in his way. He desires to drink the cup that the Father gives him. The drinking of this cup is fulfilled in Jesus' thirst on the cross. No doubt Jesus experienced physical thirst on the cross, but John's explicit mention of Jesus' words, "I am thirsty" (19:28) evokes an even deeper meaning. Jesus' thirst is related to the direct accomplishment of his work fulfilling not only the will of the Father but the Scriptures as well.

Most likely the unquoted Scripture text is from Psalm 69. This prayer is that of a person in anguish. Twice there is explicit mention of thirst: "my throat is parched" and "for my thirst they gave me vinegar to drink" (Ps 69:3, 21).

The psalm has three sections expressing lament (Ps 69:1-3, 7-12, 20-21). It is one of the most quoted psalms in the New Testament.

> Save me, O God . . .
> I am weary with my crying, my throat is parched (Ps 69:1, 3).
>
> O God of Israel . . .
> It is for your sake that I have borne reproach, that shame has covered my face. . . .
> It is zeal for your house that has consumed me, the insults of those who insult you have fallen on me (Ps 69:6, 7, 9).
>
> Insults have broken my heart, so that I am in despair.
> I looked for pity, but there was none;
> and for comforters, but I found none.
> They gave me poison for food
> and for my thirst they gave me vinegar to drink (Ps 69:20-21).

John himself has employed this psalm earlier in his Gospel. After Jesus lashed out against the money-changers and merchants in the Temple, John says that his disciples later recalled the words of this psalm, "Zeal for your house will consume me" (2:17; Ps 69:9). Later in the Gospel, Jesus cites this psalm against his persecutors, "They hated me without cause" (15:25; Ps 69:4). Though not cited in his passion narrative, John most likely has the third part of this lament in mind when he mentions Jesus' thirst on the cross (19:28; Ps 69:21). John seems to have woven sections of this psalm's expression of lament into the fabric of his Gospel. Though somewhat veiled in symbolic allusion, the unquoted last section of this threefold lament is none the less powerful in impact. Jesus dies proclaiming his thirst while bringing his work to an absolute completion. In Jesus' death, God's work and will is accomplished.

"BREAK NOT A BONE" (19:31-36)

"These things occurred so that the scripture might be fulfilled: 'None of his bones shall be broken'" (19:36).

"Now since it was preparation day, in order that the bodies might not remain on the cross on the sabbath, for the sabbath of that week was a solemn one, the Jews asked Pilate that their legs be broken and they be taken down. So the soldiers came and broke the legs of the first and then the other one who was crucified with Jesus. But when they came to Jesus and saw that he was already dead, they did not break his legs'' (19:31-33).

As John's passion narrative moves toward a conclusion, he reflects once again that the events surrounding the death of Jesus fulfill the Scriptures. John proposes two texts: "None of his bones shall be broken" (19:36) and "They will look on the one whom they have pierced" (19:37). Only the first text concerns our psalm prayer reflections since it is most likely from Psalm 34. The other text is from the prophet Zechariah.

The soldiers did not break the legs of Jesus because he was already dead. This is another indication that Jesus died on the eve of the Passover, the day of preparation as John calls it. Jewish leaders were concerned for the proper observance of the feast beginning at sundown, for this Passover was also a sabbath. It was, as John mentions, a particularly solemn feast (19:31). Because of this the leaders petitioned Pilate that the legs of those executed be broken in order to hasten their death, allowing burial before sundown. Since Jesus was already dead, the soldiers did not break the bones of his legs. John interprets this as a further fulfillment of the Scriptures.

Scriptural commentators are divided on just what text John has in mind in the citation, "None of his bones shall be broken" (19:36). Some feel it is a reference to the paschal lamb (Exod 12:46; Num 9:12), while others suggest a verse from Psalm 34 (Ps 34:20). This psalm celebrates God's protection of the just and faithful Servant. Quite possibly John has merged the two scriptural images to heighten his symbolism.

Despite the lack of consensus on the Old Testament references alluded to in John 19:36, we do know that John develops the image of Jesus as the Lamb of God. Since John does seem to favor the psalms, more than likely the text is the one from Psalm 34. The other psalms quoted in John's passion narrative are Psalm 22 and Psalm 69. They both refer to the persecution of the Just One of Israel. Perhaps John now employs Psalm 34 to develop the same thematic image. However, instead of using a lament over the sufferings of the faithful Servant, this time he employs a prayer of thanksgiving for God's protection of the Just One. If this is so, a prayer of thanksgiving is offered precisely at the moment of Jesus' death. Since John's symbolism is so rich we cannot overlook this possibility. What is most interesting, if the reference is to God's protection of the Just One found in Psalm 34, is that it is interpreted in the rich context of John's Passover story and in the light of John's use of the image of the paschal Lamb.

> Many are the troubles of the just man,
> but out of them all the Lord delivers him;
> He watches over all his bones;
> not one of them shall be broken (Ps 34:20, 21 NAB).

John has set the date of Jesus' death at the eve of the Passover, when the lambs were prepared with unbroken bones for eating in the next day's feast. He has also referred to the use of hyssop in the death scene of Jesus as a reminder of the sprinkling of the lamb's blood on the night of liberation for the Hebrews (19:28-30; Exod 12:7, 13). This linkage between Jesus and the paschal lamb would not have been foreign to early readers of Jewish background since at the time of the feast of Passover many of the readings from the synagogue Lectionary would have been about the paschal lamb and the festal regulations prohibiting the breaking of its bones. The lamb was sacrificed on a Friday, a day we have come to call Good, because on it sin was forgiven. This forgiveness was proclaimed through the preaching of the Baptist (John 1:29) and accomplished through the death of

God's only Son (19:30; 3:16). In John, both message and image unite in the death of Jesus, the Lamb of God.

Liturgy and Prayer

For present-day Christians John's passion narrative is the Lectionary selection for the Good Friday assembly. This use is documented from our earliest traditions until the present day. Today in our worshipping assembly, amid the drama of the reading of Christ's passion and the solemnity of the three-day celebration of his paschal mystery, we are drawn once again into the richness of John's meditation on Jesus' passion and death. In that telling of the passion story, we recall that Jesus suffered and died at the time of the Passover so that the Scriptures might be fulfilled.

By developing the theme of the paschal lamb, John has formed a structural inclusion with the Baptist's testimony given at the beginning of Jesus' ministry: "Here is the Lamb of God" (1:29). He has also executed an impressive crescendo for his Passover motif throughout the story line of his Gospel (2:13; 6:4; 11:15; 12:1; 13:1; 19:14). The melody, though intricate, creates a unified harmonic theme. For John, who has employed the Baptist to announce his theme and his passion narrative to express it, Jesus is "the Lamb of God who takes away the sins of the world!" This is true both in the public proclamation of John's Gospel and in the privacy of our personal prayer.

Prayer Exercises

Three Passover Stories at the Cross
- Jesus Cleanses the Temple (2:13-25)
  "Destroy this temple and in three days I will raise it up" (2:19).

- Jesus Feeds the Multitudes (6:4-59)
  "The bread that I will give for the life of the world is my flesh" (6:51).

- Jesus and the Risen Lazarus (11:17–12:2)
  "I am the resurrection and the life" (11:25).

Select one of these earlier Passover stories and reflect on it in the light of Jesus' final words at the cross, "It is finished" (19:30). As you enter into the story you have chosen, pray about how this event is an image of the work Jesus will complete in his passion. Does this reflection help you to understand the meaning of Passover in your own life?

Three Psalm Prayers at the Cross

- "They Divide My Garments" (19:23-25)
  Read Psalm 22.

This psalm is most closely associated with the passion, most often in terms of its opening line, "My God, why have you forsaken me?" John, however, employs the psalm to reflect on the dividing of Jesus' garments and the keeping of his seamless tunic in one piece. This is reminiscent of the garment of the high priest which was forbidden to be torn (Lev 21:10). Perhaps John wants us to see Psalm 22 as an extension of Jesus' priestly prayer. Read and pray over both John 17:1-26 and Psalm 22. Does praying these two texts together give you any new insights into the apostolic dimensions of Christ's passion?

- "I Thirst" (19:28-30)
  Read Psalm 69.

What aspects of Christ's passion are reflected in this psalm for you? Pray about them in the light of the text John 19:28-30. Pray with Christ in his passion, asking for the strength you need to bear whatever affliction or sorrow might be touching your life now.

- "Break not a Bone" (19:31-36)
  Read Psalm 34.

This psalm helps John join the image of God's just Servant and the paschal lamb. Pray this psalm together with John 19: 31-36. How is Jesus God's faithful Servant and lamb of sacrifice for you? Remember, both the servant and the sacrificial lamb took upon them the sins of others. Express a prayer of gratitude as you reflect on these images of Jesus—for he is the Lamb of God who has taken away the sin of the world (1:29). Because of this, Jesus is worthy of all praise and thanksgiving (Rev 5:1-14). Read Revelation 5:1-14 and pray in thanksgiving for the saving work of Jesus, the Lamb of God, accomplished on your behalf.

Recommended Reading

Brown, Raymond, S.S. *The Gospel According to John.* Garden City, N.Y.: Doubleday and Co., 1970.

Collins, Raymond. "John's Gospel: A Passion Narrative?" *The Bible Today* (May 1986).

Fuller, Reginald. "The Passion, Death and Resurrection of Jesus According to St. John." *Chicago Studies* (April 1986).

Haenchen, Ernst. *John: A Commentary on the Gospel of John.* 2 vols. Philadelphia, Penn.: Fortress Press, 1984.

Kysar, Robert. *John.* Augsburg Commentary on the New Testament. Minneapolis, Minn.: Augsburg Publishing House, 1986.

Senior, Donald, C.P. *The Passion of Jesus in the Gospel of John.* Collegeville, Minn.: The Liturgical Press, A Michael Glazier Book, 1991.

Snackenburg, Rudolf. *The Gospel According to John.* New York: Crossroad, 1982.

Talley, Thomas. *The Origins of the Liturgical Year.* New York: Pueblo Publishing Co., 1986.

Trocmé, Etienne. *The Passion as Liturgy.* London: SCM Press, 1983.

Yee, Gail. *Jewish Feasts and the Gospel of John.* Wilmington, Del.: Michael Glazier, 1989.

Chapter 6

"Alleluia!"
A Concluding Reflection

Psalm 118, with the Alleluia, is the psalm designated for the acclamation before the reading of the gospel of the resurrection on both the Vigil and the Easter feast. This psalm was originally a psalm for procession. Most likely it was a procession through the gates of the ancient Temple to celebrate the faithfulness of God who had led the people to renewed life in the covenant. Originally this psalm was connected with the feast of Tabernacles. It speaks of the worshipers dwelling in tents or "booths" as at the time of the feast. "The joyful shout victory in the tents of the just" (Ps 118:15). Jesus went up to this feast and spoke of himself as living water (John 7:10, 37).

Psalm 118 was also associated with the feast of Passover and the singing of the Alleluia or the "Hallel" psalms (114–118). This last psalm of the great hymn of praise accompanied the filling of the fourth cup of wine at the celebration of the Passover. Jesus celebrated these great songs of Israel's praise of God on the night before he died. Luke speaks of Jesus longing to celebrate the Passover with his disciples, and Matthew mentions the singing of a hymn of praise before Jesus and his disciples went out to the Mount of Olives (Luke 22:15; Matt 26:30). On these great feasts of Israel, God's people sang Psalm 118 in celebration of the Lord's constant and ever-faithful care for them. In this musical celebration they made memory of God's special bond, the covenant love God shared with them as a people.

Remembering God's Love

The covenant bond with the Lord is remembered in the story of the Exodus when Israel passed through the sea under the protection of God, entering into a new relationship with the Lord. The memory of this event is celebrated each year in the readings of the Vigil of Easter. The memory of God's covenant love for the people was always one of Israel's primary motives for singing God's praise. Every aspect of her saving history was punctuated by reflective praise of the Lord's compassionate and constant love. Psalm 136, a remembrance of creation, the Exodus, and Israel's entrance into the land of promise, celebrates the timelessness of God's love in the frequently repeated refrain, "His steadfast love endures forever" (Ps 136:1ff.). It is this same quality of God's enduring and compassionate love that is the central motivation for thanksgiving in Psalm 118.

In the central verses of this Easter psalm we are called to remember Israel's ecstatic gratitude for its deliverance through the sea. "The Lord is my strength and my might, he has become my salvation" (Ps 118:14). This praise for God, the guardian of a people called to new life, is at the heart of Israel's awareness of its covenant relationship with the Lord. "You are my God, and I will give thanks to you; you are my God, I will extol you" (Ps 118:28). These joyful phrases echo the sentiments expressed in Miriam's ecstatic song of praise recorded in the Book of Exodus. "Sing to the Lord, for he has triumphed gloriously; horse and rider he has thrown into the sea" (Exod 15:21). This song is celebrated in the Vigil service of Easter as part of the recalling of Israel's deliverance through the waters of the sea. In the extended version of this song later attributed to Moses, we find both imagery and verses that are taken up in Psalm 118. No wonder the Church has selected this psalm for the Easter celebration. "The Lord is my strength and my might . . . He has become my salvation. This is my God, and I will praise him . . . I will exalt him" (Exod 15:2; cf. Ps 118:14). "Your right hand, O Lord, glorious in power . . . Your right hand, O Lord, shattered the enemy" (Exod 15:6; cf. Ps 118:15, 16).

Celebrating God's Love

As the memory of the Exodus was at the center of Israel's self-awareness as a people, so too was praise for God's steadfast and saving love at the heart of Israel's worship. This centrality is reflected in the structure of Psalm 118 with the remembrance of the Miriam/Moses song of thanksgiving for Israel's deliverance recalled in the central verses of the psalm. The victory shouts come from those who dwell in the festival tents of Israel's people. "The Lord is my strength and my might. . . . There are glad songs of victory in the tents of the righteous. . . . The right hand of the Lord is exalted . . . " (Ps 118:14, 15, 16). These verses with their trusting reliance on God are the heart and central portion of this psalm of thanksgiving for the Lord's eternal, penetrating, and all-embracing love.

Just as the motive for praising God is placed at the heart of this psalm with the recalling of the Exodus and the consequent song of triumph, so too a command or invitation to praise the Lord is found at both the beginning and conclusion of this celebration of God's love. "Give thanks to the Lord for he is good, his steadfast love endures forever"

(Ps 118:1, 29). Like Israel's people of old, we too are called to be centered in and surrounded by God's ever-faithful love. It is our motive to praise the Lord.

In the course of celebrating this wonderful psalm of praise all people are called upon to offer unconditional praise to God. All are invited to praise: the whole nation—"Let Israel say . . . ", the priests—"Let the house of Aaron say . . . ", indeed, all who worship—"Let those who fear the Lord say . . . " (Ps 118:2, 3, 4). The reason and motivation for this invitation to praise the Lord is ushered in with the simple but eloquent word found in the title and opening word of this most appropriate Easter psalm: Alleluia, Praise God!

Alleluia! A Prayer of Memory and Celebration

Christ's passion, death, and resurrection are the new Exodus celebrated by the Church and in each Christian heart at Easter. Whether in noble public ceremonies or private personal prayer, gratitude for God's goodness echoes on our lips and in our hearts. Psalm 118 is well chosen to reflect and celebrate our awareness of a link with the past event of Israel's deliverance and our present experience of rising to an ever new life in Christ. This psalm of reflective thanksgiving gives the re-intonation of God's glorious praise at Easter a timeless expression. Alleluia, Praise God! The word says it all.

The verses of this Easter psalm sound like a meditation on the Lord's paschal mystery. The early verses seem to reflect upon a person's deliverance from suffering, a remembrance of the passion, if you will: "Out of my distress I called on the Lord. . . . All nations surrounded me. . . . They surrounded me on every side. . . . I was pushed hard so that I was falling . . . " (Ps 118:5a, 10a, 11a, 13a), but compare, "The Lord answered me and set me in a broad place. . . . In the name of the Lord I cut them off. . . . The Lord helped me . . . " (Ps 118:5b, 10b,

11b, 13b). The later verses of the psalm seem to echo the rejoicing of a person who has known deliverance from death, perhaps even resurrection: "The right hand of the Lord does valiantly. . . . I shall not die but I shall live and recount the deeds of the Lord. . . . Open to me the gates of righteousness, that I may enter them and give thanks. . . . This is the day that the Lord has made, let us rejoice and be glad in it . . . " (Ps 118:16b, 17, 19, 22, 24).

In the context of personal remembrance or public liturgy prayerful reflection on Psalm 118 is a renewed motivation to sing God's praise for Christ's paschal mystery. Joy in the resurrection of Christ inescapably involves accepting the crucial role the mystery of his passion plays in our lives. Prayerfully, we ponder the crucified Christ in order to engage in the living of his gospel. By reason of our mission as baptized believers, we make our own the words of St. Paul, "We preach Christ Crucified," of whom we proclaim, "He is risen"(1 Cor 1:23; Matt 28:6). Alleluia!

Prayer Exercises

Paul testifies to the ancient truth of Christ's resurrection (1 Cor 15:1-11)

Peter proclaims the crucified Jesus, Lord and Christ (Acts 2:14-36)

This is our faith; not an external truth but an intimate mystery bonding us with the risen Christ who was crucified. It is a simple yet awesome truth giving warmth and texture to the fabric of our lives.

Read and pray 2 Corinthians 4:5-11.

Express your wonder at the pattern of Christ's paschal mystery within your own life!

Re-read John 11:1-45 and 12:1-11

Dialogue once again with the person you asked to accompany you on the journey of your prayer experience with Christ's passion: Mary, Martha, Lazarus, or Jesus himself. Now that the journey is complete, what advice or encouragement does the person offer you? Pray about what they say.

In conclusion recite Psalm 118 with the spirit of Alleluia in your heart.

Recommended Reading

Anderson, A.A. *Commentary on the Psalms.* 2 vols. New Century Bible Commentary. Grand Rapids, Mich.: William B. Eerdmans, 1981.

Cornwell, Malcolm, C.P. *Arise and Renew: Easter Reflections for Adult Believers.* Collegeville, Minn.: The Liturgical Press, 1986.

Rogerson, J. W., and J. W. McKay. *Psalms.* Cambridge Bible Commentary. Cambridge: Cambridge University Press, 1983.

Stuhlmueller, Carroll, C.P. *Psalms.* 2 vols. Wilmington, Del.: Michael Glazier, 1983.